The Spirit of the Lord

Renewal Spirituality, Biblical Justice

and the

Prophetic Witness of the Church

ESTRELDA ALEXANDER

Seymour Press SP

The Spirit of the Lord:
The Holy Spirit, Biblical Justice, and the Prophetic Witness of the Church
©2022 by Estrelda Alexander

All Rights Reserved. No part of the book may be reproduced in any form without written permission from Seymour Press.

Cover Design by: Tim
Printed in the United States of America

Scripture quotations, unless otherwise noted are from the New American Standard Bible ©2005 by The Lockman Foundation and are used by permission.

Seymour Press
Lanham, MD

ISBN:978-1-938373-43-5
LCCN: 2020949473

Contents

Foreword i
Preface v
Introduction 1
The Case for Biblical Justice 13
Justice in the Old Testament 25
Justice in the New Testament 61
Spirituality in Movements of Renewal 83
So Great a Cloud of Witnesses 99
Prophetic Witness 141
Conclusion 193
Bibliography 201
Index 205

Dedication

This work is dedicated to my grandmother, Estavy Stubbs Douglas, who taught me to love God, the Bible and the Church, and encouraged me to be filled with the Spirit and to be bold. And to all of those who have suffered injustice and have not been able to speak for themselves or act on their own behalf. And, finally, to those who have mentored me and shaped my thinking regarding justice.

Appreciation

This book came about because Dr. Christopher House, Associate Professor of Communication Studies at Ithaca College had the courage to invite me to address the conference that pushed me to reconsider and codify my thinking on these vital issues. To him, I am forever grateful.

Dr. Sheila Robinson read through this work and offered excellent critique and assistance in editing the final manuscript.

My husband, Clem Alexander allowed me the time and space to wrestle through this manuscript.

Foreword

The theme of justice in the Bible does not center only on addressing wrongdoing or unethical behavior before God but reveals God's loving and upright character. The expression, "God is just," means God is perfectly righteous in all God's ways.[1] When we use the phrase, we are not simply speaking about how God acts, but about what God is like and who God is.

Though many Hebrew scholars inform us that the Old Testament words *"mishpat"* and *"tzedakah"* cannot be directly translated into English, a rough approximation is that *mishpat* refers to the judgment issued by a shofet (judge) involving legal rectitude according to the law. On the other hand, tzedakah refers to the righteous character of a person or a group. According to Abraham Joshua Heschel, though the terms are not identical, they must always be kept in tandem. For him, the first is a righteous mode of action, and the second is the righteous quality of an individual or group.[2] The biblical idea of justice invites us into an ethical universe in which God rules with right judgment and *hesed* love towards God's people. Justice is rooted in God's character in showing redeeming love towards God's creation.

As a consequence of the fall, humanity is prone to act selfishly, unjustly, and wickedly towards others and antithetically to our Creator. Genesis 3-6 gives us a vivid picture of a world in which sin is rampant, and humans are left to our own moral and ethical standards. In Genesis 6:5, "… the Lord saw that the wickedness of man was so great…

---

[1] Psalms 145:17.
[2] Abraham Joshua Heschel, *The Prophets*. New York: Harper Perennial Moderns Classics, 2001, 200-201.

and that every intent of the thought of his heart was only evil..." The Hebrew word for "wicked, "*rashah*," means 'guilty' or 'in the wrong,' and refers to the mistreatment of another by ignoring their dignity as created in God's image. Tzedakah justice requires more than the application of a legal remedy; it is a heart issue calling for an epistemological shift in thinking and being. For this reason, after the great flood, God called Abraham to build a people who would exemplify God's moral and ethical character rooted in justice and righteousness.[3]

The *šōfēt*, as God's administrators of justice, were to acquit the innocent, condemn the guilty, and expose false accusations and bribery. 2 Chronicles 19:7 tells us that in every city, they were to take heed not to judge for man but for the Lord, for "*there is* no iniquity with the Lord our God, no partiality, nor taking of bribes." Judges were not to show favoritism, either by taking pity on the poor or favoring the rich who sought to influence justice by paying bribes [4]. When the children of Israel demanded a King, God still required that Kings represent God's just and righteous character by taking care of the weak and defenseless and treating their subjects with dignity and fairness.

Old Testament prophets were often the unwelcomed voices and represented the conscience of God when the people were in a state of apostasy. They called out injustice and insisted that the right worship of God cannot exist without justice. The major and minor prophets all had something to say on the issue.

Even the High Priests were expected to uphold justice and righteousness in the execution of their office. They

---

[3] Genesis 12.
[4] Exodus 23:3; Leviticus 19:15.

offered sacrifices that satisfied God's justice and demonstrated God's mercy. The psalmist declares God as the lover of justice who freely offers it to us. God is Holy and set apart from all that would cause God to act with impartiality. For God's holiness is intrinsically tied to God's justice.

The life and ministry of Jesus personified this rich, Old Testament legacy. For him, justice and righteousness weren't part of a new covenant, prophetic tradition, but come out of this prophetic tradition and are the culmination or *telos* of God's reign in the world. In following his example, the role and function of the Church are to be a physical sign of God's Kingdom rule in the world. This Kingdom must be one in which *mishpat* and *tzedakah* are lived out by God's people.

Recalling the biblical foundation for justice underscores the importance of this book, *The Spirit of the Lord: The Holy Spirit, Biblical Justice, and the Prophetic Witness of the Church*. The call to stand for justice is often construed as advancing a political, social, or theological agenda. However, passionate appeals to remember the prophetic biblical tradition of *mishpat and tzedakah* not only goes to the core of our Judeo-Christian heritage. It expands our knowledge of God and understanding of what it means to be created in God's image. Alexander has been at the vanguard of this clarion call within the renewalist church tradition, and this book extends her prophetic voice.

As a biblical womanist and public theologian, she laments that the Holiness, Classical Pentecostal, and Charismatic traditions have often viewed the call for justice with suspicion. Indeed, for many renewal leaders and educators, the struggle for justice is seen through the lens of neo-Marxist or socially and politically liberal left-wing agendas. Liberation theologies, critical race theory, feminist and womanist theologies, and any cry from the margins of society are viewed as theologically liberal and radical socialism that is anti-American and unchristian.

This book brings three foundational Christian pillars to our memory to combat the anemic understanding of biblical justice often portrayed in Pentecostal and renewalist traditions. The first reminds us that justice is not the responsibility of a few voices crying in the wilderness but all our responsibility. In his 1963 letter from a Birmingham Jail, Dr. King reminded us that "[i]njustice anywhere is a threat to justice everywhere [and] [w]hatever affects one directly affects all."

The second pillar presents a biblical theology of justice drawing upon Old Testament understandings, including the concepts of *mishpat* and *tzedakah*. This pillar also develops a thoughtful New Testament theology of justice by examining key texts and ideas of its writers. The third, and perhaps most fascinating, pillar constructs a rarely employed pneumatological theology of justice. It does this in two ways. First, it discusses the role of the Holy Spirit in the work of justice. It then uncovers essential lessons about justice and injustice from the perspective of a Pentecostal heritage that relays accounts of significant contributions by our forerunners, paying particular interest to William Seymour and the Azusa Street Revival.

This book is a welcomed contribution to the ongoing conversation about Pentecostalism, the Church, and racial justice that has been going on for at least the last decade and has intensified in the past two years precipitated by the brutal killing of George Floyd. It provides the distinct renewalist, frank contribution the tradition sorely needs.

Dr. Clifton R. Clarke. President
Alliance of Black Pentecostal Scholars

Preface

My Fall 2019 keynote address entitled, "The Holy Spirit, Social Justice and the Prophetic Witness of the Church" at a secular liberal arts college re-energized my interests in the history of involvement of renewal movements in issues of justice. It also sparked an interest in producing an in-depth work to address a deficiency in understanding the issue within this tradition.

My experience as an African American woman has primarily been within multicultural renewal contexts. I have served in predominantly white mainline and Evangelical institutions of higher education and white, African American, or multicultural congregations. Though my interest has been mainly the African American classical Pentecostal context where I was raised, exposure within the broader Christian tradition, though somewhat limited, provides new ways of looking at a subject that my tradition often dismisses out of hand.

Yet, the same issues plaguing the broader society increasingly challenge renewal communities: Personal, family, and communal brokenness, economic inequality, poverty, and other concerns continue to challenge an authentic Christian witness from the Church and its leaders. This disparity leaves leaders without an adequate understanding of their vocational call to, individually and collectively, influence the cultures in which they live and serve.

Leaders and congregations base insufficient solutions to complex problems on less than adequate understandings of issues and one of two inappropriate approaches. The first sees the sole or primary benefit of Spirit-empowerment as enablement to live a personally holy life and, thus, qualify for eternal reward. This response relies on literal propositions that fail to, seriously, engage present-day culture, while negating the Holy Spirit's ongoing work in forming the contemporary Church for ministry. The second response reduces the authority of Scripture to a minimal role in influencing Christian actions and attitudes. Both approaches leave leaders ill-prepared to lodge a practical, biblical response to issues faced by their constituents, their community, and the broader society.

Some arguments in this work appeared in previous volumes but deserved reiteration to answer the deafening silence from the tradition. Though others may benefit from the argument laid out in these pages, I am speaking to Christians committed to embracing a more holistic understanding of mission within our fractured community and world. I hope this work sparks deep personal reflection, more intentional conversation, and more active participation in justice-seeking.

1

Introduction

Within the contemporary renewal community—the Holiness, classical Pentecostal, Neo-Pentecostal, and Charismatic traditions—efforts to challenge injustice and redress those who suffer under oppressive systems are often viewed with suspicion. Proponents of economic, social, ethnic, gender, or cultural liberation are often suspected by their communities of mounting narrowly defined campaigns to gain power for their constituencies at the expense of upsetting God's ordained order for the Church and society. These efforts are often perceived as radical attempts by fringe individuals or groups to infuse the core Christian message of eternal salvation with secular, ungodly agendas. Purportedly these efforts move believers from our mission to work toward the redemption of souls and their reconciliation into a saving relationship with Christ.

Some perceive struggles to obtain fundamental human rights and the dignity others consider their natural privilege antithetical to authentic biblical spirituality. Moreover, some critics claim that true spirituality dispenses with attempts to gain individual rights for the sake of keeping the "unity of the Spirit" within the Christian community. This often means, however, keeping the peace at all costs while natural and material needs of some believers go unmet and the rest of the world, figuratively at least, goes to hell.

To insinuate that enduring injustice is simply the cross of the oppressed to bear is an unfortunate misreading of Scripture or a deliberate attempt at spiritualizing the status quo. Unfortunately, this misinterpretation is too often used to keep those oppressed by violence, abuse, racial disparity, and economic deprivation from breaking free.[1] Such a narrow understanding of unity does not consider seriously that within a world besieged with all manner of tyranny, we are called to be our brother, sister, and neighbors' keeper. Further, as the parable of the Good Samaritan intimates, that neighbor might be someone who is not part of our immediate community—does not look or speak like us, or share our faith commitment. Neither does it consider that, often, bringing genuine unity requires wrestling through hard issues that unsettle seeming peace and disrupt superficial comfort, but ultimately brings true wellbeing for the entire community. Further, narrow mindsets dismiss social, economic, or gender disparity as, simply, the unfortunate, yet irreparable, consequence of the Fall. They may perceive inequality as a situation to be patiently borne as one's particular cross. Or they see providential deliverance from injustice as arriving, eventually, without disruptive human intervention, within God's preordained, largely indeterminable, timeframe. Those who hold these mindsets classify themselves as biblically faithful believers while castigating the so-called liberative efforts of other Christians as deconstructive attempts at replacing biblical faith with liberal human programs.

In his 1987 work, *Radical Liberation Theology: An Evangelical Response*, for example, missionary scholar, Raymond Hundley, found "little that is laudatory" in liberation theology. Instead, his assessment was typical of many who have never encountered the theology firsthand or have never been victims of oppressive behavior or systems. He casts it as a "theological and doctrinal revolution" that opposed "the very foundations of traditional Christian

---

[1] Kelly Palmer, A 'Cross To Bear' Means Actively Embracing The Cost Of Following Jesus, *Sojourners. https://sojo.net/articles/cross-bear-means-actively-embracing-cost-following-jesus, accessed May 11, 2021.*

doctrine," [as] "a whole new way of looking at Christian faith [and] challeng[ing] all past ways of being Christian."[2]

One student in a contemporary theology seminar at a Bible Belt, Evangelical seminary vividly nuanced this way of thinking. He interrupted the discussion, questioning how the justice issue related to the Gospel or saving souls, quickly adding that further discussion was senseless if it had nothing to do with the evangelistic endeavor.

At first, the critique was disarming, and I struggled to counter with an immediate adequate response. Yet, the encounter was so disturbing that I prepared an entire lecture for the next class session. My agitation was overshadowed by seeing the question as representing the present tenor of much of a tradition in which I have spent most of my life. It signaled a major shortcoming in the dichotomous renewal theological enterprise.

On one side, there is, what is considered, the scriptural mandate for winning and discipling those who do not know Christ and preparing them for a glorious afterlife. But the comprehension of this mandate is often attached to inattention to the lived situations of many believers—and non-believers—challenged by systemic evil, social injustice, and lack of access to a decent quality of life in this present world.

A roundtable discussion on that same campus highlights this dichotomy. A respected, local pastor of a trans-ethnic congregation attempted to bridge the political divide between diverse cultures within the renewal community. He admonished his hearers to put Kingdom principles of brotherly and sisterly love and unity above political, social, economic, or cultural differences and to refrain from using invective to characterize those with whom we disagree.

---

[2] Raymond Hundley, *Radical Liberation Theology: An Evangelical Response.* Wilmore, KY: Bristol Books, 1987.

Instead, he contended, Christians should graciously and patiently engage each other as brothers and sisters in Christ, to resolve entrenched concerns. Yet, even in this attempt to provide an objective, centered, and reasoned discourse, he referred, offhandedly, to those passionately concerned about justice as "on the left." In doing so, he immediately discredited his early statements about objectivity.

On the other hand, many who work diligently to bring about justice, seemingly show little interest for the eternal well-being of individuals they seek to redeem from temporal oppression. They abstain from using the word "sin" to characterize any individual's behavior—even when others would classify such behavior as unbiblical. Yet, they easily apply the sin label to oppressive corporate structures. These Christians, refrain from offering an apologetic for Christian faith, either seeing it as one truth—one spirituality–among many, or seeing distorted understandings of Christian faith as, somehow, complicit in oppression.

But, for renewalists, there is a third way to view issues of justice-seeking. Theologian, James Forbes and sociologists, Donald Miller and Tetsunao Yamamori describe this approach as "progressive Pentecostalism." They use this label to characterize those believers who embrace renewal spirituality while working for social change within their communities.

Forbes outlined essential requirements for providing a progressive renewal witness. First, he speaks of going beyond narrow concern for personal deliverance to embrace a holistic vision of the Spirit's work. He insists we move beyond denominational narrowness and isolation (and the narrowness of the tradition) to engage more significant tasks than can be handled alone. Simultaneously, he calls us to acknowledge the Spirit's engagement in every human activity that brings us closer to realizing the Kingdom of God. For he concludes that the Spirit is not only concerned about individual souls—"spiritual things"—but about anything affecting attainment of abundant life and liberation. Finally, he alerts us that while affirming our past spiritual experiences, we cannot limit the Spirit to traditional patterns.[3]

Miller and Yamamori speak of progressive Pentecostals as Christians who claim to be "inspired by the Holy Spirit and the life of Jesus, [while] seeking to holistically address the spiritual, physical, and social needs of the people in their community"[4] Their work and that of Forbes suggest that progressive renewal sensitivity has little to do with denominational identification. Instead, this spirituality is shared by those believers who holistically address the spiritual, physical, and social wholeness of their communities, society, and world.[5] This understanding intimates the unfruitfulness of captivity by either rigidly fundamentalist conservative social and economic agendas or an ultra-liberalism that denies the authority of the inscripturated Word of God.

While progressive renewalists' numbers are growing, they are in the minority. And, though many renewalists steer clear of describing themselves as "Evangelical," reserving the term for propositionalism, fundamentalism, and right-wing politics, progressive renewalists uphold major tenets of historical Evangelical faith. Both groups believe in the virgin birth, the deity of Christ, the efficaciousness of His atoning

---

[3] See James A Forbes, Jr., "Shall We Call this Dream Progressive Pentecostalism?" *Spirit: A Journal of Issues Incident to Black Pentecostalism* 1:1 (1977), 12-17.

[4] Donald Miller and Tetsunao Yamamori. Global Pentecostalism: The New Face of Christian Social Engagement, Berkeley, CA: University of California Press; 2007.

[5] Ibid.

work on the Cross, salvation by faith in Jesus alone, and the need for a personal experience of conversion. Most importantly for this discussion, both groups hold a high view of Scripture as the ultimate authority in matters of faith. This shared vantage point provides opportunities to engage in discussions of justice, since it is fundamentally a biblical concept and requirement.

Progressive renewalists—whether Holiness, Classical Pentecostal, Neo-Pentecostal, or Charismatic—support a more holistic understanding of the social, economic, and cultural issues impacting their congregations, communities, society, and world than does the broader Evangelical community. They also are more willing to employ a variety of tools—not solely the Bible and prayer—and to form strategic alliances with liberal Christians, non-Christians, and secular entities on common concerns.

One difficulty, however, is that some progressives classify all conservative Christians as fundamentalists without according them the same benefit of the doubt they ask for themselves. They often cast other renewalists as bringing a biblicist, literal understanding to the discussion of contemporary issues. Further, they see little chance of moving detractors to a center position and judge arguments for justice as falling on deaf ears.

In part, the problem is that these discussions start from the wrong position. Again, attempts to launch conversations from social, political, economic, or cultural arguments miss the point that justice is, essentially and primarily, a biblical matter. More importantly, active justice-seekers can fail to understand that meaningful discussions of these realities must engage the biblical imagination of hearers and speak a language they can appreciate.

So, to offhandedly question efforts to work for justice dismisses the witness of Scripture. The pursuit of justice by God's people is not a new idea; it is, again, a biblical matter. Throughout its texts, God's people—Israel and God's new people—the Church, are repeatedly reminded of God's standard of social, as well as personal, holiness and expected to live by it.

Old Testament prophets and writers of the Pentateuch, History, and Wisdom Literature dealt with the subject. Each genre speaks of God's standard and requirement for justice. Likewise, New Testament writers did not neglect the issue. The Gospels—the life and ministry of Jesus among his disciple and the Jewish community—witness the need to uphold justice. Likewise, the Apostles and other New Testament writers address justice in their narratives and epistles; even the book of Revelation speaks of it.

Yet, a false dichotomy prevents the renewal community from effectively assaulting genuine injustices and creates a deafening silence signaling tacit complicity in allowing things to remain as they are. Consequently, young people, sensing the need to seek justice, feel inclined to pursue it outside the faith community. While leaders decry this unfortunate situation, we do little to show that the movement is relevant. And so detractors gravitate to groups that embrace their visionary pursuits while dismissing any need for spiritual accountability.

Misconceptions of the tradition's total unconcern about the present reality, entire focus on otherworldly pursuits, and lack of contribution to the justice conversation miss a history of generations who have addressed injustice. Sermons and writings, participation in civic concerns, and forging alliances that work for the benefit of their communities is as much a part of the witness of some renewalist leaders as is spiritual matters. Though many have sought to rescue individuals as much from the hell of oppressive temporal existence as from eternal hell, their efforts have been largely overlooked in unfortunate characterizations of renewalist spirituality. These women and men tackled problems that seemed intractable, discovering warrant for their actions in Scripture, and understanding Spirit-empowerment as God-given enablement for tearing down strongholds of oppression and injustice.

Revisiting their stories, re-visioning their actions, and rehearing their voices emboldens contemporary renewalists to mine their witness for courage to address ongoing oppression. Moreover, their stories underscore how we can hold to important doctrinal values without sacrificing a commitment to justice.

Hearing from this great cloud enables us to discern what renewal spirituality can contribute to the present situation of oppressed people. We can ask what it meant for them and what it means for us that Jesus is the Christ? What it meant and what it means that we are saved? What it means to claim a supernatural measure of God's empowerment? And, how that empowerment enables us to negotiate oppressive terrains that do not grant complete dignity to those fully created in the same image of God as those in places of power. Moreover, we can hear how Spirit-empowerment fosters rejection of an idea of a God that capriciously discriminates against any branch of God's created humanity in favor of another.

The founding event of the renewal tradition—the Azusa Street Revival—launched a prophetic movement that took God's call for justice seriously and broke down oppressive barriers. Indeed, many early Pentecostal leaders lodged vehement apologetics for seeking justice. Though by no means the majority voice in succeeding generations, the proclamation of justice was unmistakably present through preachers such as William Seymour and Charles Harrison Mason, activists such as Arthur Brazier and Herbert Daughtry, proto-womanist Ida Robinson, and scholars like Bennie Goodwin, Leonard Lovett, Robert Franklin, and Robert Beckford.

None viewed oppression as simply a cross to bear for the cause of Christ. Rather, they understood suffering under oppression as part of systemic evil wielded by the "prince of the power of the air, the spirit that is now working in the sons of disobedience"[6] to wreak havoc on the created order. More importantly, each felt called to resist that spirit and work toward the community's liberation.

In pursuing justice, religious individuals and communities, including local congregations, denominations, and parachurch organizations, generally employ one of three approaches—tempered by their particular world view—to confront the challenges facing our communities: accommodation, reform, or activism.

Accommodationist responses acknowledge the hopelessness of bringing about any actual resolution to injustice. Rather, purveyors assist their community to make the best of a bad situation. Historically, this is where many renewal communities fall. Unfortunately, such an approach has left many adherents more than prepared to get into heaven while they struggle to get through the next day. It has made them "happy prisoners" in circumstances and systems for which they see no earthly adjudication; they pray that accounts will be settled in their favor in the hereafter. Many revivalistic communities employ this approach, as they are

---

[6] Ephesians 2:2.

careful not to be drawn off track from what they see as their God-ordained mission to save souls.

Reform responses seek to integrate the community into the larger society or with those who impose injustice in ways that are, at least minimally, acceptable. These responses don't disturb the comfort of the perpetrating community while providing them with a sense that *something* is being done. Indeed, the expectation is that by coming up to the standards of the larger community and making themselves more acceptable, the victim of oppression will eliminate their "deserved" distress. Mainline religionists' primary contribution to ameliorating oppression is reform approaches through acts of benevolence. These ease the offeror's conscience, but don't overturn the values on which injustice rests.

Activist responses attempt to alter unjust systems by questioning the elements that form them or showing a more just and fair means of attacking them. Scripture clearly informs us that we are not simply battling against individual human ploys —flesh and blood, but we are fighting to dislodge systemic realities—the rulers, powers, and forces of darkness in this world, as well as the spiritual forces of wickedness in the heavenly places.[7]

Renewalists who choose to employ either activist approach have three spiritual weapons at their disposal. Pneumatological unction is the Spirit-empowered agency— the God-given anointing—to act on behalf of those who suffer any manner of oppression. It informs the believer that the injustice that grieves God's heart should also grieve those who claim to have God's Spirit indwelling them. Pneumatological urgency is the compelling, Spirit-driven sense of need to act on behalf of justice without regard to

---

[7] Ephesians 6:12.

expediency. The endowment of the Holy Spirit as the inner force impels prophetic voice and action to encourage or bring about a resolution. Prophetic audacity enjoins us to speak boldly on behalf of God for those who cannot speak for themselves. It enables us to stand in places forsaken by a Christian church that has chosen comfort and conformity over vision.

In the end, Christian believers cannot be among those who see injustice only as it is and ask why it exists? Instead, we must employ, what Old Testament scholar and theologian, Walter Brueggemann, calls, "prophetic imagination"[8] to envision the temporal manifestation of the Kingdom of God as we have never experienced it and ask, "why not?"[9] We are called to work toward that spiritually discerned Kingdom for we have as a yearning deep within our souls for that which has yet to break into our fallen reality. Our motivation for involvement in the justice project must be to conform ourselves to the image of Christ.

---

[8] See Walter Brueggemann, *The Prophetic Imagination*. Minneapolis: Fortress Press, 1978.
[9] Bernard Shaw, *Back to Methuselah: A Metabiological Pentateuch*. New York: Brentano's, 1921.

2

The Case for Biblical Justice

Despite where one stands on the issue, sincere Christians cannot simply dismiss the idea of justice as a current fad that goes in and out of vogue as circumstances change. Those who misunderstand the subject regard attempts to engage justice as, largely or entirely, a secular or worldly endeavor. They artificially bifurcate the sacred and the profane—the temporal and the spiritual creating a cleavage between justice and biblical faith. Such a stand is antithetical to an authentic renewal spirituality which makes no such distinction, but sees God, the Creator of all humankind, as concerned about the entire human situation. As Scripture relates, before each person is born, God considers[1] us, and Jesus, as our high priest, is touched by the real concerns of all of our lives.[2]

For those on either side of the discussion, the idea of justice can quickly become a trendy topic that leads to a contentious conversation. Yet, while the term "justice" may seem the catchword of the day, both in the religious and secular realms, the need to engage such matters has solid scriptural grounds. With God, justice is not a peripheral idea or passing concern; as part of God's nature and integral to God's being in Creation, it is central and timeless. Scripture reminds us that "… all God's ways are just; God is one… of faithfulness [who is] without injustice."[3]

Contemporary definitions, however, sometimes obscure the biblical significance of the concept. Further, attempts to craft meanings that either thrust the issue entirely into the

---

[1] Jeremiah 1:5.
[2] Hebrews 4:15.
[3] Deuteronomy 32:4.

secular realm or create overly spiritualized paradigms do little service to authentic efforts to understand the complex circumstances, associated with the subject. Therefore, the challenge of situating a Christian perception of justice in its proper sphere must begin with exploring common understandings of various iterations of the word.

The umbrella term, justice, addresses the many ways oppressive socio-economic, political, legal, religious, and environmental mechanisms keep individuals and communities from full human flourishing. It has come to mean the fair, equitable treatment of individuals and groups that frees them from subjugation to others in these areas. Justice deals with deconstructing dualisms (i.e., male/female, white/non-white, rich/poor; haves/have nots, first world/two-third world, gay/straight) as the grounds for inequitable treatment of individuals or communities; or for denying them emancipation from suppressive social norms.

Christians who hold a high view of the authority of Scripture can easily reject this understanding. On its face, it appears to conflate issues about which members of the faith community hold vastly different moral convictions. While using the Bible as the lens to make ethical decisions, identifiable camps see vastly different messages. Further, since each holds their interpretation as correct, it is almost impossible to reach satisfactory compromises on what constitutes just handling of many issues.

Terminology regarding the concept of justice can be problematic. What is fair? What is equitable? And by whose standards? What does it mean to deconstruct an understanding? And, more importantly, what understanding(s) do we put in its place? To some, the very ideas seem threatening. What are we saying when we speak of oppressive social norms? By what measure do we determine if oppression is inflicted from outside or is a self-inflicted, unfortunate situation.

Some sincere Christians disallow any definition of justice that ascribes blame or responsibility to one group for others' injurious circumstances. In their view, righteousness—defined as being in right relationship with God—is the simple recipe for flourishing. Many contend that the failure of an individual or group to flourish is primarily—at its root—due to being out of proper relationship with God. Further, they contend that any human attempt to rectify what might appear to be injustice would be out of the will of God. This understanding ignores the reality that many devout Christians are victims of injustice through no fault of their own. Though we might, offhandedly, refer to their situation as an accident of birth—race, ethnicity, gender, class, caste, or intellectual or physical ability—some are relegated to positions of disadvantage while others are afforded a degree of privilege.

Just as importantly, these misguided perceptions obscure the biblical understanding that God so loved the entire world and that every member of the human family is the object of God's love. Accordingly, every person created in God's image deserves dignity and respect, along with the opportunity to thrive in an environment that allows that image to be reflected and discerned by others. Yet attempts to raise individual or community awareness about the issue provoke other concerns. For often, the very notion of consciousness-raising frequently associated with doing justice brings with it connotations of promoting misleading ideology. It is interpreted as indoctrination into ideas that run counter to biblical truth.

Types of Justice

While the term 'justice' is overarching and inclusive, justice issues encompass distributive, restorative, procedural, retributive, and environmental arenas. Each has specific implications for individuals and communities, yet the idea of fairness is entwined in all of these. Further, if we read Scripture deeply, taking the time to sit with its implications for our present reality, each of these is found in its pages. Indeed we cannot read Scripture honestly without coming to terms with its requirement for justice at every turn.

Distributive, or economic, justice relates to fairness in disseminating the material resources people and communities need to live with a reasonable level of comfort. It refers to the equitable–rather than equal–allocation of societal assets and assumes that resources will be divided fairly. The concept also assumes that equal work should provide individuals with an equitable material gain or the ability to acquire resources. Such justice is absent when equal work fails to produce equitable outcomes or when an individual or group receives disproportionate resources at the expense of others. The idea of distributive justice assumes that no individual or group is excluded from access to the commodities required for living within this reasonable level of comfort. Or, no individual or group endures undue hardship in acquiring these resources, and no artificial barriers are erected that preclude access to them.

Restorative justice seeks to make whole those who have suffered unfairly from some form of injury by calling the wrongdoers into account and putting things back as they should be. It emphasizes repairing the harm caused by oppressive behavior or systems. True restorative justice acknowledges that wrongdoing does not only impact the offender and victim, but the entire community experiences a loss. It also acknowledges that wrongdoing is not imposed by those we would identify as "the hardcore element," but that, instead, much of it appears to be soft or "victimless" injury whose harm is not immediately, nor easily, identified. Rather its harm may be long-term and deep-seated and stem from practices that, on their surface, may seem benign.

The idea of restorative justice generally brings to mind such instances as reparation for slavery or adequate sentencing for an offender while making the victim whole. However, its principles can apply where individuals or groups have been locked out of fair opportunity to compete for societal assets such as education, employment, or safe communities. When such justice is not administered even-handedly, it encourages conflict between the offending individual or institution and the offended individual or group. Restorative justice acknowledges if there is to be healing and peace, those who do wrong need healing as well.

Relatedly, retributive justice involves the appropriate level of punishment of offenders regardless of their standing within the community. Its primary intent is to dissuade perpetrators from continuing disruptive behavior. But it also seeks to discourage others from future wrongdoing. When a penalty is applied unevenly, punishment becomes revenge that is more severe than mere reparation for victims. Its objective becomes exacting "an eye for an eye" to force the perpetrator to suffer to a greater extent than the crime deserves. Or harsh penalties become a mechanism for keeping a target group in check by introducing measures of fear and control. However, authentic retributive justice precludes the motivation of vengeance, ensuring that the punishment is not graver than the crime.

Procedural justice refers to implementing legal systems and processes that ensure unbiased treatment of each individual and that rules that govern society are impartially and consistently applied to all parties. Such justice calls those carrying out neutral processes that allow affected parties a voice in the process. When those affected believe in the fairness of a process, they are likely to accept the outcome, even when disagreeing with it. Procedural justice, however, assumes proper action by both those who formulate processes and those who carry them out. Further, it presumes that as common understandings of fairness are based on agreed-upon values, morality, and conventions, the formulator's autocratic will is not imposed upon the ruled. Moreover, it assumes that such procedures or laws will be equally applied to all regardless of their social identification.

Environmental justice entails the equitable treatment of all people regarding the burden and benefits of consuming the earth's resources. It realizes that everyone is a stakeholder in preserving these resources and that no group can rightly deplete them for their own comfort when such use diminishes, or eliminates, access for entire other groups. Understandings of environmental justice suggest that those most negatively affected by the misuse of resources are trapped at the lower end of the socio-economic spiral and most likely to experience the immediate costs. Yet, they concede that environmental abuse has detrimental consequences for all of Creation, regardless of where an individual stands.

Promoters of environmental justice recognize that everyone desires to live in a safe and healthy community that is free of life-threatening conditions. However, they acknowledge that, whether by conscious design or institutional neglect, human actions and decisions disproportionately expose some to hazards that reduce the quality of their material lives and force them to bear a more significant burden simply because of who they are or where they live.

In sum, biblical justice involves the notion that every person or group within a society deserves fair economic, political, and social opportunity, irrespective of race, gender, caste, creed, geography, or religion. Furthermore, it insinuates that every human family member is an equal stakeholder in its thriving. Therefore, living in a socially just way precludes discrimination or oppressive attitudes and actions based on any common identifier. Instead, a biblically just individual or community does away with artificially imposed, socially identifiable barriers and provides equal openings for every individual to develop their inherent human qualities and fully flourish.

Progressive and conservative believers rarely agree on the nature or place of the liberative agenda within the Christian project. Instead, they attribute the structured inequality that leads to deep disparity in real-life situations to different causes. Such disagreement means that each faction sees the other's views about causes and cures for injustice with suspicion and disdain. And each side ascribes to the other, what they see as, unbiblical motivation.

Progressive Christians tend to blame injustice solely on the social context, believing that individuals are oppressed by historical or contemporary forces that are generally beyond their control. They note that individuals are born into situations over which they have no control; they don't choose their race or gender, or the socio-economic class into which they are born. They do not determine whether they are born into a free or oppressive political system. However, progressives contend that birth circumstances have implications for how justice is meted out. And, they hold that those who are fortunate to have been born on the "right" or privileged side of the scale are likely to disproportionately inherit the resources required for flourishing.

For progressive Christians, those born into a degree of privilege are obligated to consider the plight of the less fortunate. They argue that we are all our brother's and sister's keepers. They contend, moreover, that, as members of one human family, every man or woman is our brother and sister. However, one danger is that progressives can adopt a reductionism that attributes all misfortune to injustice.

This view makes little room for personal culpability or individual responsibility for any lack the individual or group encounters. Still, we cannot deny the role of imposed strictures such as lack of access to adequate medical care, underfunded education, and unfair employment opportunities. These common societal cues that one is somehow inadequate follow the identified group from the cradle to the grave. But since these impediments are not readily observable or experienced by others, privileged group members often deem them minimal or non-existent.

On the other hand, social conservatives are more likely to point to the root of disparity as, almost entirely, resulting from personal responsibility. They assume that individuals can help themselves and improve their situation no matter the obstacles they face. They point to those parts of Scripture which encourage hard work and frugality and discourage a sinful or immoral lifestyle as the cause of material want.[4]

Further, some Christians propose a narrow interpretation of justice that reduces it to benevolence—individual or group actions towards singular needs, usually among those considered more deserving. These well-intentioned believers

---

[4] For example, several passages in Wisdom Literature, especially Proverbs and, less prominently, Song of Solomon and Psalms suggest this sentiment.

see no need to uproot the underlying causes of injustice. For, they see the sources of situations as either an unfortunate and substantially irreparable consequence of the Fall or as beyond the ability of human responses to alter significantly. Or alternatively, they see victims as, somehow, implicated in bringing about the circumstance and resistant to taking the necessary steps for its amelioration.

As a theologian, rather than a biblical scholar, one might consider me ill-prepared to make a compelling case for a biblical foundation for doing justice. Yet having been formed within classical Pentecostalism, with its high regard and heavy reliance on Scripture as the rule for personal and corporate morality, I have always attempted to imbibe and live out a biblical base for any theology I espouse.

Such a theology recognizes both the structural and individual actions at play in oppressive situations. For Scripture acknowledges that personal causes can lead to disparity in resources. For example, slothfulness, lack of wisdom in managing material resources, and failure to plan can lead to scarcity. Further, the Bible roundly decries such attitudes and actions. Instead, it urges individuals to adopt habits such as industry, good attitudes towards work, and thrift that provide the necessary resources and lessens the possibility of suffering lack.

Yet, Scripture also clearly speaks of unjust, oppressive situations caused by the corrupt political or economic actions of those in power. It portrays circumstances in which those who control the means of production and distribution use uneven standards. It castigates judges who employ unequal measures for rendering rulings. It condemns forcing individuals into servitude because of situations beyond their doing. Moreover, it condemns misuse of the earth's resources and disregard for the impact of overindulgence that leads to dire consequences for the rest of creation.

Scripture also prescribes how God's people should relate to victims of injustice, rarely emphasizing who is at fault. For, regardless of its source, the Bible calls those who love God and seek to be faithful to God's requirement of justice to show mercy and work toward remedies. As contemporary Christians—people of the Book—then, no matter where we stand on the political, social, economic, or cultural issues that confront our society, any authentic discussion regarding justice must start with the understanding that the call for justice has its foundation there.

The Bible is not only concerned about our relationship with God. It adamantly challenges our hypocrisy in proclaiming love for God whom we have never seen while showing no love for the brother or sister who may be different from us but is still part of God's so loved world. That love is more than a "kum ba yah" moment or a warm fuzzy feeling. It involves deep concern for their welfare and flourishing. Not only does Jesus and the apostles make this point explicitly throughout the New Testament, but several Old Testament texts point out the inconsistency of such a posture.

3

Justice in the Old Testament

Hebrew Scripture represents a word spoken to and about a people who experienced both sides of oppression. The Israelites were often under attack or victimized by succeeding empires, including the Egyptians, Philistines, Babylonians, Assyrians, Persians, and Chaldeans. Nevertheless, God was mindful of the injustice they suffered and repeatedly sent deliverance through Spirit-empowered men—and women. Moreover, the prophets foretold of a hopeful future and an ultimate deliverer who would come to live among them.

But God's people also were often purveyors of injustice; they regularly had to be admonished that such behavior was unacceptable since Israel was chosen as much to bring blessing to the nations as to receive blessings. Though God, through the prophets, continually proclaimed their responsibility to uphold their covenant obligation to do justice, the community repeatedly failed.

Significantly, two Old Testament terms convey the concept of justice. The first, mishpât (מִשְׁפָּט), occurs, in various forms, more than 200 times in these texts. Its most straightforward usage means to make things right or rectify a wrong and describes caring for those who cannot adequately care for themselves. Philosopher and theologian, Nicholas Wolterstorff identifies these persons as "the quartet of the vulnerable"—widows, orphans, immigrants, and the poor.[1] World Vision, the Christian outreach organization, identifies a quintet of the weak, vulnerable, marginalized,

---

[1] Nicholas Wolterstorff, *Justice: Rights and Wrongs*. Princeton, NJ: Princeton University Press, 2010.

disenfranchised, or disinherited.[2] The term connotes a justly ordered community where corporate and interpersonal behavior values fairness, so each person has human dignity and flourishes. Repeatedly, the prophets railed against the absence of mishpat among abusive leaders and those who mistreated the poor or stranger. And they declared that God was neither oblivious to nor willing to let injustice go unpunished.

The second term, *"tzedakah,"* (צדקה) is usually translated as being righteous or just. Yet, immediately, contemporary readers encountering the word "righteousness" think of personal piety, such as chasteness, moderation in use of intoxicating substances, persistence in prayer, or participation in public worship. More fully, however, the term reflects a life of right relationships with God, neighbor, the broader society, and the whole creation. It speaks of how individuals fairly and impartially conduct everyday dealings with family, community members, and the larger society.

Taken together, Scripture pairs the two terms, mishpat and tzedakah —justice and righteousness—personal and communal holiness—over three dozen times in a way that best conveys the contemporary concept of justice. Notably, the biblical paradigm for authentic justice and righteousness is always triangular. It not only encompasses our relationship with God but includes the relationship between God, ourselves, and our community. Indeed, Scripture insists that God does not honor worship that fails to consider complicity in the plight of the oppressed. From the biblical vantage point, the answer to the question, "Am I my brother's keeper?" is a resounding "Yes!"

---

[2] World Vision, "What Does Social Justice Really Mean?" https://www.worldvision.org/blog/social-justice-really-mean.

No portion of what we know as Hebrew Scripture–the Law, History, Wisdom, or the Prophets–fails to speak of justice in terms of mishpat, tzedakah, or both. Even a cursory examination of these texts reveals the importance of these issues to God and how integral they were in the nation's everyday life.

The Law

The Pentateuch–the first five books of Hebrew Scripture which contemporary Christians refer to as "The Law"–is a compilation of material related to Israel's earliest history and the history of God's covenant making with the community. These accounts reveal that, from the beginning, humankind was created for relationship with both God and other members of the human family. They inform us that any injury that disrupts this relationality can be traced, at its root, to some form of injustice. So, in essence, such an act is sin. This foundational understanding sets the stage for exploring God's requirement for justice as an integral component of God's character and ideal for Creation. Acts of injustice, by definition, are breaches of the intended relationship between God, the individual, and the community.

We do not go far into the biblical text, however, before we discover that, as a result of the Fall, injustice became interwoven into the fabric of human interaction. Indeed, within the second generation, we find its graphic depiction when Cain killed Abel.[3] Though God calls him into account for his action, Scripture does not shy away from reporting that from that moment, injustice, in its various forms, continued to be a part of the human situation.

---

[3] Genesis 4:1-14.

The book of Genesis is replete with instances of interpersonal injustice. For example, Sarah's abuse of Hagar, her handmaiden, displayed a wanton lack of consideration for the welfare of the other.[4] Sarah insisted that her husband use Hagar as a surrogate to produce the child she appeared incapable of having. But when that happened, she became angrily jealous and treated Hagar unjustly.

Jacob's unfair partiality among his sons engendered envy from the siblings that led to Joseph's mistreatment at their hands. Though the idealist had done nothing more than share his dream with them. And for that, he was sold into Egyptian slavery.[5] Judah's mistreatment of his daughter-in-law, Tamar, is another instance.[6] Though the two had engaged in intercourse, three months later, he accused pregnant Tamar of prostitution and attempted to discard her by ordering that she be put to death.

In Exodus, the Egyptian enslavement of the children of Israel exemplifies the kind of injustice the nation would, repeatedly, endure. First, the Israelites were subjected to unfair labor practices when forced to make bricks without straw. They suffered harsher mistreatment when Pharaoh decided to carry out genocide by declaring that firstborn Hebrew male babies be put to death. God was not pleased and sent deliverance. As God's emissary, Moses was sent to Pharaoh to deliver the message, "Let my people go." When he remained unheeded after several attempts, Moses took on his new role as deliverer to lead the people out of bondage. As God began to lay out the covenantal law with the newly freed children of Israel, justice was at its heart.

---

[4] Genesis 37:3-16.
[5] Genesis 37:18-36.
[6] Genesis 38.

You shall not wrong a stranger or oppress him, for you were strangers in the land of Egypt. You shall not afflict any widow or orphan. If you afflict him at all, and if he does cry out to Me, I will surely hear his cry; and My anger will be kindled, and I will kill you with the sword, and your wives shall become widows and your children fatherless.

If you lend money to My people, to the poor among you, you are not to act as a creditor to him; you shall not charge him interest. If you ever take your neighbor's cloak as a pledge, you are to return it to him before the sun sets, for that is his only covering; it is his cloak for his body. What else shall he sleep in? And it shall come about that when he cries out to Me, I will hear him, for I am gracious...[7]

Though neither word for justice appears in this portion of Scripture, the ideal is not missing. Indeed, several incidents speak of God's concern that the people deal fairly with each other. For example, in Numbers, we witness the first incident of ethnic discrimination and God's response to it. Moses' siblings Aaron and Miriam spoke against him "... *for he had married a Cushite woman,*[8] –a woman of color. And God lets them know that such behavior was unacceptable. Moses reiterates the inheritance of the Levites, the purpose of the six cities of refuge, and how the children of Israel were to conduct judicial hearings of accused murderers. Both the plight of the innocent and the welfare of the accused were to be considered. The book ends as the children of Israel prepare to enter the Promised Land.

In this book, Moses reminds the people how they were to conduct their legal affairs regarding the inheritance of land

---

[7] Exodus 22:21-27.
[8] Numbers 12:1.

within the tribes. In the narrative, the five daughters of Zelophehad approached Moses and the leaders with a just plea for a share in the land, presenting the argument, "Let not our father's name be lost to the clan." When Moses brought their case to God, who answered, "The plea of the daughters of Zelophehad is just," the women received the right to inherit their father's land.[9]

As the Law was codified in Leviticus, God reiterated the standard for how God's people should conduct themselves toward others in their midst. Among the several clauses dealing with almost every aspect of the community's life were explicit commandments governing the just treatment of both their fellow persons and the stranger—non-Israelite—who for some reason was sojourning among them:

> *"Do not pervert justice; do not show partiality to the poor or favoritism to the great, but judge your neighbor fairly"*[10]
>
> *Do not use dishonest standards when measuring length, weight or quantity. Use honest scales and honest weights, an honest ephah and an honest hin...*
>
> *When a foreigner resides among you in your land, do not mistreat them. The foreigner residing among you must be treated as your native-born. Love them as yourself...*[11]
>
> *You shall thus observe all My statutes and all My ordinances and do them...*[12]

---

[9] Numbers 27: 1-11.
[10] Leviticus 19:15.
[11] Leviticus 19:33:34.
[12] Leviticus 19:37.

You shall have one standard for stranger and citizen alike...[13]

In Deuteronomy, Moses restates the requirement for justice, showing God to be the one who "*... executes justice for the orphan and the widow, and shows His love for the alien by giving him food and clothing.* Further, God explicitly indicated the expectation that the children of Israel would show the same kind of justice in their dealings with each other.

If there is a poor man with you, one of your brothers..., you shall not harden your heart, nor close your hand from your poor brother; but you shall freely open your hand to him, and shall generously lend him sufficient for his need in whatever he lacks... and [if] you give him nothing; then he may cry to the Lord against you, and it will be a sin in you.[14]

Yet these passages rarely assess blame for an individual's lack—determining whether it is self-inflicted or imposed by an external set of circumstances. Neither does it delude us to believe that, in a fallen world, we can entirely eradicate deprivation. Instead, it insists that since "*... the poor will never cease to be in the land.*" the people of Israel must *"freely open [their]hand"* to them. [15]

And God's people must always deal with each other fairly, making sure in dealings to:

... appoint judges ... [that] shall judge the people with righteous judgment. You shall not distort justice; you

---

[13] Leviticus 24:22.
[14] Deuteronomy 15:7-8.
[15] Deuteronomy 15:11.

shall not be partial, and you shall not take a bribe, for a bribe blinds the eyes of the wise and perverts the words of the righteous.[16]

They were prompted, repeatedly, that their actions were to reflect the justice that is God's nature. They were to understand that everything they possessed had been graciously bestowed by the same Lord who delivered them from Egyptian bondage. So, they were to show gratitude by extending that same graciousness to others. As formerly oppressed strangers in Egypt, they were to treat the stranger in their midst as they desired to be treated. But, as these texts vividly inform us, Israel often fell short of these ideals.

Historical Books

The twelve historical narratives—Joshua, Judges, Ruth, 1 and 2 Samuel, 1 and 2 Kings, 1 and 2 Chronicles, Ezra, Nehemiah, and Esther—cover approximately one thousand years of Israel's history, beginning with the conquest of Canaan and ending with the return from Babylonian captivity. In these books, the successes and failures of mediating the demands of the Law is, again, a repeated theme.

These texts show occasions when other nations oppressed Judea and Israel and God wrought deliverance. Sometimes this was through miraculous intervention; at other times, God used courageous individuals such as Samson, David, or Deborah and Gideon to bring liberation. But the texts also speak of times when the nation did not uphold God's standard toward others, and God judged both rulers and people for unfair dealings.

---

[16] Deuteronomy 16:18-19.

These books speak of constant skirmishes both within and between the nations. For there was rarely a period when there was complete, peace either within their own borders or with their neighbors. The Ethiopians, Philistines, Ammonites, Arameans, Assyrians, Babylonians, Persians, Moabites, and Meunites were among its enemies.[17] But Israel and Judea sometimes allied with different powers against each other.

In the story of the siege of Jericho in Joshua, we are ultimately dealing with a question about God's justice. By human standards, we can question the morality of slaughtering an entire community. Yet, this is an instant in which God uses Israel to enact judgment on an utterly corrupt society that regularly and violently abused its most vulnerable members. The hard questions raised in this scenario bring to mind the contemporary issue of whether there is such a thing as 'just war.' Further, we must ask who, besides God, has the right to determine when this concept can rightly be invoked.

The book of Judges portrays a period between the death of Joshua and the establishment of a kingdom when a generation came about who "did not know the Lord, nor even the work which He had done"[18] Because of this ignorance, they became a law unto themselves and brought about a time of social and political upheaval. Twice we are informed that since there was no king, "everyone did what was right in his own eyes."[19] The narrative of the cyclical pattern of the nation's moral behavior expresses God's justice in two important ways. First, it shows the necessity of God's judgment for violations of God's standards that damage divine-human and personal relationships. Secondly, we see God's fairness

---

[17] See for example, 1 Samuel 11, 1 Kings 15, 2 Kings 6, 20.
[18] Judges 2:10.
[19] Judges 17:6, 21:25.

in judging Israel when they violate Law and other nations when they oppress Israel.[20]

The portrayal of the Levite who turns his concubine to the men of Gibeah, of the tribe of Benjamin to be unmercifully raped is a graphic display of dual injustice.[21] It raises issues of the tie between justice and law, and suggests that the excessive punishment meted out as the near-total destruction of the Benjamites is itself an incident of injustice. It alerts us that it is possible to wage a 'just war' in an unjust manner.[22]

While this book does not rehash specific commands about which the people are already aware and speaks mostly about idolatry, we can insinuate that injustice came about,

> [b]ecause this nation ha[d] violated [God's] covenant
> which God commanded their fathers, and ha[d] not
> listened to [God's] voice.[23]

1 and 2 Samuel, 1 and 2 Kings, and 1 and 2 Chronicles continue to lay out the nation's history. They portray the ethical successes and failings of both kings and ordinary people, and these books are full of oppressive dealings among God's people, court intrigue, and "wars and rumors of war." The story of the two nations reminds us that even those who claim to represent God's higher standard regarding justice seldom are entirely obedient to God.

Grave breaches of justice are played out in the life of Israel's most beloved king, who Scripture calls *"a man after God's own heart."*[24] To cover up his adultery—and the injustice

---

[20] See Athena E. Gorospe "Introducing Judges" *Tecarta Bible*. https://tecartabible.com/share/1126/506.

[21] Judges 19: 22-30.

[22] Judges 20.

[23] Judges 2:20.

[24] 1 Samuel 13:14.

of sexual abuse of a king over his subject—David devised a murderous plan to have Uriah slaughtered in battle. The Prophet, Nathan, called him out, raising the king's consciousness about overstepping his ethical boundary, and he is judged. In another graphic example, David left his daughter, Tamar, without redress for the rape suffered at the hands of her half-brother, Amnon. David abdicated his responsibility to render justness by failing to call his son, the perpetrator, into account.[25] His oldest son and successor, Solomon, bound the Israelites to unreasonable taxation and a heavy burden of servitude to pay for his extensive building projects.[26] And his son and successor, Rehoboam, made the tax burden even heavier.[27]

Ahab and his Phoenician wife, Jezebel, abused their authority and military might to dispose of the prophets violently and oppress God's people. Then, wishing to acquire their neighbor's vineyard to expand his gardens, Ahab arranged Naboth's execution on the false charges of blasphemy against God and the king.[28] In reading these narratives, we must be mindful, that in many instances, the Bible is descriptive rather than prescriptive. It is honest about the consequences that come about because of failure to be just. And nowhere is this more explicit than in the portrayal of the end of Ahab and Jezebel.[29]

Yet, we also find examples of God's people faithfully working to bring about justice. In the book of Nehemiah, for example, God's people organized to redress unfairness in the community when Nehemiah, cupbearer to the Persian King, returned to Jerusalem to rebuild the city wall. During

---

[25] 2 Samuel 13.
[26] 1 Kings 9-11.
[27] 2 Chronicles 8:1-8.
[28] See I King 16-21 and II Kings 9.
[29] 2 Kings 9:33.

construction, the people cried out because a drought had forced them to take loans to buy food and pay taxes. When debtors were unable to repay, moneylenders attempted to seize everything they owned: fields, vineyards, orchards, and even their children. But Nehemiah called a "great assembly" to hold the charlatans accountable, forcing them to restore what they had taken.

Nehemiah understood that without justice, the Jews would have no future. He succeeded in convincing the nobility to remit the debts and restore the forfeited fields of the poor.[30] On doing so, he also restored economic justice in the land, admonishing the wealthy for taking advantage of their less fortunate brothers and sisters.[31]

His colleague, Ezra, "*had set his heart to study the Law of the Lord, …and … teach his statutes and rules in Israel.* [32] For him, this included God's standard of justice. The king, **Artaxerxes, commissioned Ezra to**

> *… appoint magistrates and judges so that they may judge all the people who are in the province… And whoever does not comply with the Law of your God…, judgment is to be executed upon him strictly, whether for death or for banishment, or for confiscation of property or for imprisonment.*[33]

The book of Esther is the only biblical narrative that does not mention God's name, nor the word justice. Nevertheless it tells of a clear injustice pending in Ahasuerus kingdom. His

---

[30] 1 Kings 21:1-16.
[31] Nehemiah 6:6-13.
[32] Ezra 7:10.
[33] Ezra 7:25-28.

cupbearer, Haman, uses his political position to persuade the king to order the destruction of all the Jews in the empire:

> *Letters were sent by couriers to all the king's provinces to annihilate, kill, and destroy all the Jews, both young and old, women and children..., and to seize their possessions as plunder.*[34]

Yet, in the end, Esther's efforts to bring deliverance to her people prevail, for we learn that,

> *... they hanged Haman on the wooden gallows which he had prepared for Mordecai...* [35]

Within the poignant story that unfolds in the book of Ruth, we see an application of the idea of just community. While the concept of justice is never explicitly spelled out in the legal sense, the ideal of bringing about family or communal well-being through voluntary acts of justness is very much a part of the story. Naomi and her daughter-in-law, Ruth are left at the generosity of the kinsman-redeemer who shows them mercy much as God shows to us, and in doing so enters into the ongoing story of the unfolding of salvation history.[36]

The Psalms

One of the most loved divisions of Scripture deals with every facet of the human experience to deepen our

---

[34] Esther 3:13.
[35] Esther 7:10.
[36] Boaz takes Ruth to be his wife and the two become part of the ancestral blood line of Jesus. See Matthew 1:1-17 (especially 1:5).

relationship with God. The Psalms explore every emotion: joy, gratitude, worship, victory, defeat, sorrow, grief, and self-pity. But they also relay God's reaction to those experiences; the issue of justice is no exception. In the first division of the book, we are already comforted with the knowledge that

> *The wicked ...,*
> *are like chaff which the wind blows away.*
> *Therefore the wicked will not stand in the judgment...*
> *[and] the way of the wicked will perish.*[37]

The book details the methods of those who of foster injustice. Psalm 10, for example, explicitly speaks of how in their pride,

> *the wicked hotly pursue the afflicted*[38]

> *His mouth is full of curses and deceit and oppression;*
> *Under his tongue is mischief and wickedness.*
> *He sits in the lurking places of the villages;*
> *In the hiding places he kills the innocent;*
> *His eyes stealthily watch for the unfortunate.*
> *He lurks in a hiding place as a lion in his lair;*
> *He lurks to catch the afflicted;*
> *He catches the afflicted when he draws him his net.*
> *He crouches, he bows down,*
> *And the unfortunate fall by his mighty ones.*[39]

The same Psalm calls forth God's righteous intervention on behalf of those who are oppress:

---

[37] Psalms 1:4-6, *see also*, Psalms 37.
[38] Psalms 10:2.
[39] Psalms 10:7-10.

Arise, O Lord; O God, lift up Your hand.
Do not forget the afflicted.

You have seen it, for You have beheld mischief and vexation to take it into Your hand. The unfortunate commits himself to You;

You have been the helper of the orphan.

Break the arm of the wicked and the evildoer,
Seek out his wickedness until You find none.

O Lord, You have heard the desire of the humble;
You will strengthen their heart, You will incline Your ear
To vindicate the orphan and the oppressed,
So that man who is of the earth will no longer cause terror.[40]

The call for the Lord's deliverance from oppressors reverberates throughout this hymnal.

How long will you judge unjustly
And show partiality to the wicked?...

Vindicate the weak and fatherless;
Do justice to the afflicted and destitute.

Rescue the weak and needy;
Deliver them out of the hand of the wicked.[41]

---

[40] Psalms 10: 12, 14-15, 17-18.
[41] Psalms 82:2.

Repeatedly, God's character as one who "watches over strangers, orphans, and widows is reiterated, for we are told that, *the wicked will perish before God* who is *"a father of the fatherless and a judge for the widows."*[42] Moreover, as the book nears its end, the Psalmist leaves the audience with hope when he tells us that,

The Lord watches over strangers;
He supports the fatherless and the widow,
But He thwarts the way of the wicked.[43]

Wisdom Literature

If we see the four books—Proverbs, Job, Lamentations, and Ecclesiastes—emphasizing understanding and the attainment of wisdom for all areas of life, including our relationships with God and one another, we can glean from them instruction on justice.[44] Their reminder that righteousness—faithfully living out our responsibility to God and the exhibition of just relationships with others—results in prosperity and deliverance from suffering.[45] *It is the blessing of the Lord that makes rich"*[46] it tells us, not the unjust schemes we devise. Further, it declares that,

much wealth is in the house of the righteous..."[47] and *[w]hoever oppresses the poor shows contempt for their Maker, but whoever is kind to the needy honors God*[48]

---

[42] Psalms 68:2b, 5.
[43] Psalms 146:9.
[44] Bruce V. Malchow, "Social Justice in the Wisdom Literature" *Biblical Theology Bulletin* 12:4, (1982), 120-124.
[45] Proverbs 13:21.
[46] Proverbs 10:22.
[47] Proverbs 15:6.
[48] Proverbs 14:31.

While these insights run counter to our contemporary cutthroat, dog-eat-dog culture, it is the standard by which Christians must assess their faithfulness to God. So, while God does not condemn wealth, in this sagacious depository, it shows that the two paths to personal or corporate enlargement lead to very different ends. So though prosperity can result from righteous living, God disparages wealth accumulated by oppressing others.

Lamentations informs us that God is never unaware and "does not approve" when oppression is carried out. For the Lord sees every instance in which unrighteous persons,

> *... deprive a man of justice*
> *In the presence of the Most High,*
> *[or] defraud someone in his lawsuit—*[49]

It isn't that God does not hear us when we cry out for redress from our oppressors or that God is powerless to act on our behalf. Rather, God desires to grant our tormentors the same grace and mercy to which we are privy. God desires restoration rather than retribution—reconciliation rather than revenge.

Ecclesiastes again confirms that we live in a world filled with injustice, but that *"God will judge both the righteous and the wicked."*[50] It reaffirms the truth that God is not oblivious to the plight of those who suffer injustice, for as the writer tells us God,

> *... looked... at all the acts of oppression which were being done under the sun. And ... saw the tears of the oppressed*

---

[49] Lamentations 3: 35-36.
[50] Ecclesiastes 3:17a.

and that they had no one to comfort them; and power was on the side of their oppressors...[51]

The book alerts us to the reality that the wickedness and oppression we see in our contemporary society is not, at all, something new, and tells us therefore that,

[i]f you see oppression of the poor and denial of justice and righteousness in the province, do not be shocked.[52]

The Book of Job explores the question of why good people sometimes endure senseless suffering while God, seemingly, stands idly by. Job starts out as a man who is righteously rich and blessed of God. But, early in this account, everything of importance was taken from him—his livestock, his property and the lives of his children.

When Job questioned the cause of his suffering—why he was oppressed, his friends, Eliphaz, Bildad, and Zophar had over simplified, yet incorrect responses. They counseled him that it was because of his sin.[53] That is the way some Christians view those who are subject to injustice. These Christians see oppression as somehow the fault of the oppressed. This theology of divine retribution portrays a God that only allows calamities on the wicked and simply punishes those who sin. It is commonly accepted by some Christians and leaves them with a rationale for not offering assistance.

For they use biblical passages such as this as proof texts to insist, as Job's detractors, that,

---

[51] Ecclesiastes 4:1.
[52] Ecclesiastes 5:8.
[53] See Job 4:7-8; 8:20; 11:14-15, 17; 22:5-9.

... the rejoicing of the wicked is short,
... the joy of the godless [is] momentary...

He perishes forever like his refuse;
Those who have seen him will say, 'Where is he?'
He flies away like a dream, and they cannot find him;
Like a vision of the night he is chased away.
The eye which saw him sees him no longer,
His bones are full of his youthful strength,
But it lies down with him in the dust...

As to the riches of his trading,
He cannot even enjoy them...
He does not retain anything he desires...

Therefore his prosperity does not endure.
In the fullness of his excess he will be cramped...

The increase of his house will disappear;
His possessions will flow away on the day of His anger.
This is a wicked person's portion from God,
The inheritance decreed to him by God."[54]

The Prophets

The prophetic tradition of Hebrew Scripture not only alerts us to God's high standard for justice, but, again, reminds us of God's awareness of misdeeds and attention to ensure that those who practice them are held accountable. Israel's prophetic tradition spanned six hundred years, beginning with Samuel in the mid-1000s BCE, throughout the

---

[54] Job 20: 5-29.

monarchy, and into the postexilic period around the mid 400s BCE. During this period, God's spokesmen transmitted messages between the divine and earthly realms. Repeatedly, they rebuked the nation for unfaithfulness to God and mistreatment of those most in need. Still, because of mercy and grace, the nation is never entirely forsaken.

Though they are referred to as the major and minor prophets, the single difference is the length of their discourses. Whether they addressed the Northern kingdom, the Southern kingdom, or both, they were preoccupied with indicting kings, priests, other prophets, and an entire people for covenant disobedience. Yet, at the same time, they spoke comfort to the nation bound to God by that covenant.

The Major Prophets

These men:[55] Isaiah, Jeremiah, Ezekiel, and Daniel cover a significant time span and present a wide array of messages. Their longer books present broad, even global, implications.

The prophet Isaiah lived in the period just after the northern tribes of Israel were destroyed by the Assyrians and injustice was rampant in Judea. He echoes the same complaint with the Southern Kingdom that God earlier lodges against their Northern counterpart.

> *Woe to those who enact evil statutes*
> *And to those who constantly record unjust decisions,*
>
> *So as to deprive the needy of justice*
> *And rob the poor of My people of their rights,*

---

[55] Though five women are described as prophets in the Old Testament– Miriam, Huldah (2 Kings 22:14, 2 Chronicles 34:22), Deborah (Judges 4:1-5:31). Noadiah (Nehemiah 6:14), and Isaiah's wife "the prophetess" (Isaiah 8:3), there is no discourse regarding justice recorded for any of them.

So that widows may be their spoil
And that they may plunder the orphans[56]

Cry loudly, do not hold back;
Raise your voice like a trumpet,
And declare to My people their transgression
And to the house of Jacob their sins.

Yet they seek Me day by day and delight to know My ways,
As a nation that has done righteousness
And has not forsaken the ordinance of their God.
They ask Me for just decisions,
They delight in the nearness of God.

'Why have we fasted and You do not see?
Why have we humbled ourselves and You do not notice?'

Behold, on the day of your fast you find your desire,
And drive hard all your workers.
Behold, you fast for contention and strife and to strike with a wicked fist.

You do not fast like you do today to make your voice heard on high.
Is it a fast like this which I choose, a day for a man to humble himself?
Is it for bowing one's head like a reed
And for spreading out sackcloth and ashes as a bed?
Will you call this a fast, even an acceptable day to the Lord?

---

[56] Isaiah 10:1-2.

Is this not the fast which I choose,
To loosen the bonds of wickedness,
To undo the bands of the yoke,
And to let the oppressed go free
And break every yoke?

Is it not to divide your bread with the hungry
And bring the homeless poor into the house;
When you see the naked, to cover him;
And not to hide yourself from your own flesh?

… remove the yoke from your midst,
The pointing of the finger and speaking wickedness,
And if you give yourself to the hungry
And satisfy the desire of the afflicted.[57]

So, despite their profession of true worship, it is evident that the Lord was not unconscious of their unrighteous acts and, for that reason, repudiated their claim. So, early in his proclamation, the prophet would say to the people

Learn to do good; Seek justice,
Reprove the ruthless, Defend the orphan,
Plead for the widow.[58]

And later, we find him, repeating his strong warning against God's people:

Justice is turned back,
And righteousness stands far away;
For truth has stumbled in the street,

---

[57] Isaiah 58:1-7; 9b-10a.
[58] Isaiah 1:17.

And uprightness cannot enter.
Yes, truth is lacking;
And he who turns aside from evil makes himself a prey.
Now the Lord saw, and it was displeasing in His sight that there was no justice.[59]

The prophet's message was pointed and straightforward. As God's anointed, Isaiah understood his role as bringing recognition of individual responsibility to act to bring about justice when he proclaimed,

The Spirit of the Lord God is upon me, because the Lord has anointed me to bring good news to the afflicted; God has sent me to bind up the brokenhearted, to proclaim liberty to captives and freedom to prisoners.[60]

The prophet speaks of a God who love[s] justice; [and] hate[s] robbery and wrongdoing. [61]

One hundred years later, Jeremiah lived during a time leading up to the carrying away of the southern tribes of Judea into Babylonian bondage. He did not mince words, but confronts the people about the chastisement they would receive for their unfair dealings. For, he says people are found in the nation who,

... excel in deeds of wickedness; [and] do not plead the cause, The cause of the orphan, that they may prosper; And they do not defend the rights of the poor.[62]

---

[59] Isaiah 59:14–15.
[60] Isaiah 61:1.
[61] Isaiah 61:8a.
[62] Jeremiah 5:28.

Jeremiah entices his hearers with a promise from God of a peaceful existence if they,

> ... *truly amend [their] ways and... deeds, ... truly practice justice between a man and his neighbor,... do not oppress the alien, the orphan, or the widow, and do not shed innocent blood...* [63]

But because the people are prone to persist in their injustice, God tells them through the prophet,

> ... *I will give their wives to others, their fields to new owners; Because from the least even to the greatest, everyone is greedy for gain; from the prophet even to the priest everyone practices deceit.* [64]

Jeremiah also directly confronts the King of Judea with words from the Lord:

> ... *Administer justice every morning; And deliver the person who has been robbed from the power of his oppressor,* [65]

> ... *Do justice and righteousness, and ... do not mistreat or do violence to the stranger, the orphan, or the widow; and do not shed innocent blood in this place.* [66]

> *Woe to him who builds his house without righteousness And his upper rooms without justice,*

---

[63] Jeremiah 7:5.
[64] Jeremiah 8:10.
[65] Jeremiah 21:12b.
[66] Jeremiah 22:3.

Who uses his neighbor's services without pay
And does not give him his wages,[67]

And do justice and righteousness?
Then it was well with him.
He pled the cause of the afflicted and needy;
Then it was well.
Is not that what it means to know Me?
Declares the Lord.
But your eyes and your heart
Are intent only upon your own dishonest gain,
And on shedding innocent blood
And on practicing oppression and extortion[68]

Ezekiel marries righteousness and justice and declares on God's behalf that,

> ... *if a man is righteous and practices justice and righteousness... [and does not oppress anyone, but restores to the debtor his pledge, does not commit robbery, but gives his bread to the hungry and covers the naked with clothing, if he does not lend money on interest or take increase, if he keeps his hand from iniquity and executes true justice between man and man, if he walks in My statutes and My ordinances so as to deal faithfully–he is righteous and will surely live,"*[69]

At one point, Ezekiel admonishes rulers as responsible for oppression within the nation. He admonishes them,

---

[67] Jeremiah 22:13.
[68] Jeremiah 22:15-17.
[69] Ezekiel 18:5-9.

> *You have become guilty by the blood which you have shed,*[70]

> *The alien they have oppressed in your midst; the fatherless and the widow they have wronged*[71]

Though the book of Daniel does not explicitly use the language of justice, it portrays King Darius of Babylon as a fair and just ruler. Darius had no clue who would be the first victim of his edict against prayer to another deity, so after signing a decree, he came face-to-face with its effects. In continuing to pray to Jehovah, Daniel became the edict's first violator so was thrown into the lion pit.[72] Despite Darius' unsuccessful efforts to circumvent the statute, he expressed confidence that Daniel's God had power to preserve the prophet alive.[73]

After a sleepless night, the king hurried to the pit to find Daniel unharmed. As retribution, he had Daniel's accusers and their families thrown into the same pit and, eager to right the wrong, ordered that people throughout his kingdom worship Daniel's God.[74]

The Minor Prophets

Eight of the twelve minor prophets—Hosea, Amos, Jonah, Micah, Habakkuk, Zephaniah, Zechariah, and Malachi—explicitly address injustice. Rather than speak directly of the issue, however, Haggai addresses Israel's and Judea's disobedience to God's Law, and that Law, as we have seen, includes sanctions against the oppression of others. Joel, Obadiah, and Nahum make interesting detours as they speak

---

[70] Ezekiel 22: 4a.
[71] Ezekiel 22: 7b.
[72] Compare Acts 5:29.
[73] Daniel 6:9-17.
[74] Daniel 6:18-27.

of the Judgment of Israel's enemies and the ultimate vindication of the land. These Minor Prophets reinforce the message of their major colleagues that ritual activity, no matter how elaborate, divorced from attention to justice is unacceptable.

Though Hosea paints the major sin of Israel as idolatry—worshipping other gods and disregarding the tenets of God's law, he clearly perceives the connection between disloyalty to God's commands and the treatment of others.

For there is no faithfulness, nor loyalty,
Nor knowledge of God in the land.
There is oath-taking, denial, murder, stealing, and adultery.
They employ violence, so that bloodshed follows bloodshed.[75]

Joel's prophesies concern the coming *"day of the Lord"*[76]—a time of both justice for God's enemies and mercy for those who repent of their sins. For the prophet speaks of God's ultimate justice when *"everyone who calls on the name of the Lord will be saved."*[77]

This sentiment resounds with another of Isaiah's contemporaries when Amos reiterates God's adamant demand for justice. He, too, insists that God requires right treatment of others rather than empty, ingenuine worship rituals and he pronounces God's indictment:

I hate, I reject your festivals,

---

[75] Hosea 4:
[76] Joel 2:1.
[77] Joel 2:32a

> Nor do I delight in your solemn assemblies.
> Even though you offer up to Me burnt offerings and your grain offerings, I will not accept them; And I will not even look at the peace offerings of your fatlings.
> Take away from Me the noise of your songs; I will not even listen to the sound of your harps.
> But let justice roll down like waters
> And righteousness like an ever-flowing stream.[78]

Amos lists the acts of oppression: imposing heavy rent on the poor, exacting tribute of grain from them, distressing the righteous, accepting bribes, and turning aside the poor in the gate.[79] It is hard to read this book and not conclude that the Lord is moved when the weak and helpless are crushed by the powerful. Amos presents his listeners with concrete images of those who tamper with scales,[80] violate the slave girl,[81] or make exorbitant demands.[82] He reports that merchants and wealthy landowners are dishonest and greedy for more money and power. Specifically, he indicts people for "sell[ing] the righteous [into slavery] for money and the needy for a pair of sandals."[83]

Amos does not claim to be either "a prophet [or] the son of a prophet," though he stands within that tradition. To make matters worse, he was an outsider from the Southern Kingdom who preached in the Northern Kingdom where he appeared out of touch with projections of what promised to be a bright future. Moreover, the society to which his message was targeted was at its peak. Trade had rapidly developed

---

[78] Amos 5:24.
[79] Amos 5:11-12.
[80] Amos 8:5.
[81] Amos 2:7.
[82] Amos 2:6-7, 5:1.
[83] Amos 2:6, 8:6.

during a generation of peace, causing a rich and powerful merchant class to emerge. Together with the property owners and royal court, they made up an exclusive elite—a small group of wealthy, proud, luxury-loving, self-indulgent people. Yet the marginalized poor masses were mistreated for their amusement.[84] In harsh words for the elite, he called the women *"cows"* because of their *"crushing oppression of the poor and needy."*[85] He insists greedy, conspicuous consumption was the root of their depravity.

Obadiah addresses the nation of Edom, Israel's neighbor and sometime enemy, because of their detestable, insolent disregard for God's people.

> *Because of violence to your brother Jacob,*
> *You will be covered with shame,*
> *And you will be cut off forever.*
> *"On the day that you stood aloof,*
> *On the day that strangers carried off his wealth,*
> *And foreigners entered his gate*
> *And cast lots for Jerusalem—*
> *You too were as one of them.*
> *"Do not gloat over your brother's day,*
> *The day of his misfortune.*
> *And do not rejoice over the sons of Judah*
> *In the day of their destruction;*
> *Yes, do not boast*
> *In the day of their distress.*[86]

Obadiah declares with poignant clarity, the judgement that will come upon unrepentant Edom:

---

[84] Amos 7:14.
[85] Amos 4:1.
[86] Obadiah 10-12.

All the people allied with you
Will send you to the border,
And the people at peace with you
Will deceive you and overpower you.
They who eat your bread
Will set an ambush for you…
"Will I not on that day," declares the LORD,
"Eliminate wise men from Edom,
And understanding from the mountain of Esau?
Then your warriors will be filled with terror, Teman,
So that everyone will be eliminated from the mountain of Esau by murder.
Because of violence to your brother Jacob,
Shame will cover you…"[87]

Jonah's story is a tale of ethnic[88] prejudice. His concept of justice contradicts God's. So he is angry that God dares to love and forgive another group of people other than the people of Israel. Unfortunately, Jonah can't get past the past. He is stuck on viewing Nineveh as an enemy city and holding out hoped that, just maybe, God will let them die.[89] He wanted, what he saw as, justice, but God reminded Jonah that, aligned with His character, mercy and grace is extended to those who turn from their wickedness,

Should I not also have compassion on Nineveh, the great city in which there are more than 120,000 people, who do

---

[87] Obadiah 7-11.
[88] The concept of race is not present is Scripture.
[89] This is inferred in Jonah 4:2.

not know the difference between their right hand and their left, as well as many animals?[90]

God insinuates to Jonah that God will always restore a whenever a nation is penitent. Further God admonishes the prophet that God's people should be willing to extend that same grace and mercy, when oppressors truly repent.

But more than a century later, Nahum also addressed Nineveh, because the dreaded enemy has backed away from their repentance and again oppressed God's people. He forewarns of their coming destruction because of wanton ungodliness and cruel treatment of God's people, and admonishes this powerful nation they are no match for "the Lord who will *"by no means leave the guilty unpunished."*[91]

This city of violence was known for the brutal treatment meted out to its captives. The prophet called Nineveh, ... *the bloody city, completely full of lies and pillage*[92] He further, admonishes that those who have suffered at their hands are waiting to hear of God's righteous judgment against them.

All who hear about you
Will clap their hands over you,
For upon whom has your evil not come continually?[93]

Indeed, as Micah, like his contemporary, Isaiah, instructs, that injustice is extremely distasteful to God:

With what shall I come before the Lord
And bow myself before the God on high?

---

[90] Jonah 4:11.
[91] Nahum 1:3.
[92] Nahum 3:1.
[93] Nahum 3:19.

Shall I come to Him with burnt offerings,
With yearling calves?
Does the Lord take delight in thousands of rams,
In ten thousand rivers of oil?
Shall I present my firstborn for my rebellious acts,
The fruit of my body for the sin of my soul?
He has told you, O man, what is good;
And what does the Lord require of you
But to do justice, to love kindness,
And to walk humbly with your God? [94]

Habakkuk, too, lodges a vigorous rebuke against Israel and, again, entreats God to correct the nation for recklessly mistreating others:

How long, Lord, have I called for help,
And you do not hear?
I cry out to You, "Violence!"
Yet you do not save.
Why do you make me see disaster,
And make me look at destitution?
Yes, devastation and violence are before me;
Strife exists and contention arises.
Therefore the Law is ignored,
And justice is never upheld.
For the wicked surround the righteous;
Therefore justice comes out confused. [95]

However, the manner God used to accomplish that correction aroused vehement protest from Habakkuk.

---

[94] Micah 6:6-8.
[95] Habakkuk. 1:2–4.

*Why do You look favorably
At those who deal treacherously?
Why are You silent when the wicked swallow up
Those more righteous than they?*[96]

The prophet was uncomfortable with the idea that a righteous God would resort to using the wicked Chaldeans to chastise God's people. But he presents those who cry out for justice with an important lesson in that as in every other arena, God's standard for judging and recompensing justice is different than ours. Further, Habakkuk's message, like the narrative of Jonah, reminds us that God's justice is restorative, not retributive. God seeks to return all of Creation to the intimate relationality for which we were created.

Zechariah strongly makes the Lord's case for justice when he admonishes the people, first, about what they should do to bring *peace within their gates*:

Dispense true justice and practice kindness and compassion each to his brother;[97]

… speak the truth to one another; judge with truth and judgment for peace in your gates.[98]

He then reproves them about what they should not do, *for God hates such actions*. According to him, Israel must not,

… oppress the widow or the orphan, the stranger or the poor; and do not devise evil in your hearts against one

---

[96] Habakkuk 1:13b, see through 2:1.
[97] Zechariah 7:9.
[98] Zechariah 7:10.

another, ... devise evil in your heart against another, ... [or] love perjury...[99]

Zephaniah teaches us that God's justice not only addresses the wrongs among individuals but is the yardstick for establishing and measuring the rightness of a society. Speaking to the citizens of Jerusalem and by inference the nation of Israel, Zephaniah declares,

Her leaders within her are roaring lions,
Her judges are wolves at evening;
They have no bones to gnaw in the morning.
Her prophets are insolent, treacherous men;
Her priests have profaned the sanctuary.
They have done violence to the Law.
The Lord is righteous within her;
He will do no injustice.
Every morning He brings His justice to light;
He does not fail.
But the criminal knows no shame.[100]

Finally, Malachi alerts us to the reality, that injustice is as likely to occur in the privacy of the home as within the public arena. For he specifically denounces misogynist attitudes and actions of husbands and declares that God,

has been a witness between you and the wife of your youth, against whom you have dealt treacherously,

---

[99] Zechariah 8:17.
[100] Zephaniah 3:3-5. Many versions render the word, criminal as unjust or unrighteous.

though she is your marriage companion and your wife by covenant.[101]

Reprimanding husbands that they don't "deal treacherously" against the wife of their youth, he says,

I hate divorce... and him who covers his garment with violence[102]

The prophet joins his colleagues in pointing out that God's patience with the haughtiness of injustice can be stretch to the limit, when he says,

You have wearied the LORD with your words... In that you say, "Everyone who does evil is good in the sight of the LORD, and He delights in them," or, "Where is the God of justice?"[103]

And he assures us that God is not unable to bring about an accounting that,

... will be a swift witness against ... those who swear falsely, and... oppress the wage earner in his wages, the widow and the orphan, and ... turn aside the alien ...[104]

For behold, the day is coming, burning like a furnace; and all the arrogant and every evildoer will be chaff...[105]

---

[101] Malachi 2:14.
[102] Malachi 2:16.
[103] Malachi 2:17.
[104] Malachi 3:5.
[105] Malachi 4:1.

Finally, Malachi sums up the entire matter of justice by bringing the Israelites back to the command that should have set the tone for all their attempts to come to terms with an live out a God-honoring standard:

> *Remember the Law of Moses My servant, the statutes and ordinances which I commanded him in Horeb for all Israel.*[106]

It's easy for contemporary Christians to dismiss discussions of Old Testament justice as outdated. Yet, Jesus reminds us that "all the Law and the prophets "are summed up in two commandments: "love God with all your heart, and love your neighbor as yourself." And he makes it clear that you cannot authentically do the former without consistently doing the latter. Further, Jesus broadened the understanding of neighbor as more than just a member of our cultural, ethnic, or religious enclave. In doing this, he successfully refuted any insinuation that the Old Testament concerns for justice contained in these volumes are irrelevant or a secondary consideration for New Testament believers.

Moreover, Paul insists that *all Scripture*—not just our favorite, comforting, and personally world-affirming passages, is

> *inspired by God and is profitable for teaching… reproof… correction… training in righteousness; so that the man of God may be adequate, equipped for every good work.*[107]

The apostle's injunction challenges us not to ignore portions of the sacred text as simply an unnerving, social

---

[106] Malachi 4:4.
[107] 2 Timothy 3:16-17.

invention. These texts teach us the biblical meaning of righteousness and justice, reprove misguided notions of the subject, and correct failure to oppose oppression. And, if we pay attention, train us to follow God's justice-seeking methods, and equip us to be effective in doing so.

4

Justice in the New Testament

Justice is no less important in the New Testament than in Hebrew Scripture. As this section of the Bible opens, the Israelites are, again, an oppressed people. Under Roman rule, they are looking for the Messiah—a political leader who will extricate them from their situation of heavy taxation, lack of political rights, and fractured religious identity. After centuries of captivity, they hoped God would send this liberator to restore them to prominence. So, the idea of justice was essential to this community.

Jesus and Justice

Jesus was not what the Jews expected or hoped for. Instead, though He was aware of the political situation, He did not urge insurrection against the tyrannical political power structure but, instead, made himself subject to it. Yet, He railed against religious hypocrisy and bigotry. Further, He urged his hearers to exercise justice within the community, be peacemakers[1], seek their neighbor's well-being,[2] hunger and thirst after justice,[3] and live out the mandates of God's Kingdom in their present reality as if it had already unfolded.[4] Though it can mean either, New Testament translators almost exclusively render the Greek word "dikaiosune" and its derivatives as "righteousness." For example, in the King James Version,[5] the translation as justice only occurs ten

---

[1] Matthew 5:9, Jas 3:17-18.
[2] Matthew 22:39.
[3] Matthew 5:6.
[4] Matthew 6:10.
[5] The text preferred by many more conservative Christians.

times. It is never translated this way in the New International Version, and in the New American Standard Version,[6] it is one out of ninety-one. Yet, the Greek term correctly associates the concept of righteousness with that of justice. It stems from the term "dikaios" meaning "equity of character and action" where the stress on equity (impartiality, fairness) and action implies the concept of justice.

In the broad sense, the term refers to being in a righteous condition acceptable to God by exhibiting integrity, virtue, purity of life, rightness, and correct thinking, feeling, and actions toward others. In a narrower sense, it connotes justice—the virtue that renders what is rightly due to each person. Yet God's just nature and heart are so integrally linked to God's righteousness that the original Greek meaning denotes the complexity of God's character as revealed in the Old Testament "tzedakah." When rendered with its fuller meaning, the term provides a clear portrait of Jesus' mission, for Paul tells us that,

> *God made him who had no sin to be sin for us, so that in him we might become the righteousness (and justice) of God.*[7]

Moreover, we get a fuller picture of who Christians are to be, for in his admonition to his young protégé, Paul warns Timothy to,

> *Flee the evil desires of youth, and pursue righteousness (and justice), faith, love, and peace, along with those who call on the Lord out of a pure heart.*[8]

---

[6] The closest popular translation to the original text of Scripture.
[7] 2 Corinthians 5:21.
[8] 2 Timothy 2:22.

Western connotations of justice miss this point by pairing its meaning strictly with legal systems, since ideas condemnation, and punishment do not convey the New Testament notion of a God who is full of grace and mercy. Jesus did not come to impose a legal code. Instead, He offered a fully restored relationship to God and our fellow persons. He brought us into a new life flowing from within and guided by a Spirit-transformed heart to see the prerogative of justice in the law of love. Indeed, his idea of righteousness (justice) went beyond what the Law required. Repeatedly He admonished, "you have heard it said (in the Law)..., but I say,[9] encouraging his hearers to work from an internal sense of justice that cared as much about the welfare of another as oneself. Yet still, too many Christians equate justice with law-and-order, failing to see Jesus' imperative for the liberation of individuals. They miss the New Testament pairing of justice with mercy to reflect God's Kingdom on earth. Compassion and generosity are what justice should look like in the world.[10]

This understanding calls for a rereading of Scripture to see connections between righteousness and justice. In so doing, we are not adding to the word. We are simply returning to the original meaning that Jesus' hearers understood before modern, politicized interpretations were imposed upon the text. So when we read, *"seek first his kingdom and his righteousness,"* without compromising the integrity of the text's meaning, we can add, "and justice," *and all these things will be given to you as well.*[11] We can also rightly

---

[9] Matthew 5:21, 27, 33, 38, 43
[10] Jessica Nicholas, "Why Can't I "See" Justice in the New Testament? God Loves Justice. November 18, 2018. *http://www.godlovesjustice.com › blog › 2018/10/3017.*
[11] Matthew 6:33.

interpret those who hunger and thirst for justice [12] as the true meaning of that text.

Yet, for the time being, we should know that the doing of justice will result in persecution. When we read, "Blessed are they which are persecuted for justice's sake: for theirs is the kingdom of heaven," [13] Jesus links the consequences of his followers' work for justice with the Old Testament prophets[14]—but promises God's vindication. He calls them to a justice that is more than superficial, admonishing that "except your justice shall exceed [that] of the scribes and Pharisees, ye shall in no case enter into the kingdom of heaven."[15]

Matthew reiterates God's concern for authentic overtures of justice over insincere acts of piety when he relates Jesus' strong rebuke to the scribes and Pharisees. God is not impressed by some Christian circles who downplay justice while highlighting ritual morality. He confronts the same scribes and Pharisees for their superficiality with harsh words and called them,

> … *hypocrites! For you tithe mint, dill, and cumin, and have neglected the weightier matters of the law: justice and mercy and faith"* [16]

For, biblical faith is rooted in justice and righteousness that flows from the heart of God. It seeks to make all things whole, bringing them into intimate relationship with God, all of humankind, and the entirety of Creation. This faith is not a naïve nod to the status quo. On the contrary, it rejects even discreet attitudes or actions that threaten to truncate such

---

[12] Matthew 5:6.
[13] Matthew 5:11.
[14] Matthew 5:12.
[15] Matthew 5:20.
[16] Matthew 23:23.

wholeness and intimacy, acknowledging that it is "out of the heart that the mouth speaks."[17]

In Jesus' exemplary prayer, "your kingdom come on earth as it is in heaven,"[18] the coming of this Kingdom to earth was to reflect the wholeness and intimate relationship intended for us in Creation. Acts of justice were to be how his followers showed the world what heaven looks like. Yet, even among them, this vision of the Kingdom is clouded by the sin represented in the Fall.

While Isaiah claimed the mantel of anointing for himself, he also pointed to the One in whom it would be more fully vested. Jesus boldly claimed his fulfillment of the prophet's proclamation when He stood in the Temple and declared,

> *The Spirit of the Lord is upon Me, because He anointed Me to preach the gospel to the poor. He has sent Me to proclaim release to the captives, and recovery of sight to the blind, to set free those who are oppressed.*[19]

This was a revolutionary statement in a world that excluded people based on religious and cultural heritage, age, race, and gender. Yet, in Jesus' affirmation of his identity, as in his actions within the community, He confronts us with the reality that ordinary Christians who claim to be full of God's Spirit are called to be revolutionary. Those who have been devalued in the world's eyes should find family and a sense of worth among God's people, who should constantly uplift, include, and value those that society discards.

---

[17] Luke 6:45.
[18] Matthew 6:10.
[19] Luke 4:18.

For, as Spirit-empowered people—people of renewal—we claim that the same Spirit of the Lord that rested on Isaiah then Jesus has indwelled and rested upon us. We assert that this endowment by the Spirit of God provides us with the power to act as Jesus acted. This claim takes on new relevance as a metaphor for bringing the liberative good news to the materially poor, the emotionally brokenhearted, those who are captive to the exploitation of others, blinded by fear, or those oppressed by unjust social and economic systems.

This assertion is not an obligation we can lightly dismiss. For as Jesus' discourse demonstrates, God will hold each of us accountable for our failure to do whatever we can, whenever we can, and wherever we can to ameliorate injustice:

> *But when the Son of Man comes... All the nations will be gathered before Him; and He will separate them from one another, as the shepherd separates the sheep from the goats; and He will put the sheep on His right, and the goats on the left.*
>
> *Then the King will say to those on His right, 'Come, you who are blessed of My Father, inherit the kingdom prepared for you from the foundation of the world. For I was hungry, and you gave Me something to eat; I was thirsty, and you gave Me something to drink; I was a stranger, and you invited Me in; naked, and you clothed Me;... sick, and you visited Me... in prison, and you came to Me.'*[20]

As the discourse indicates, no act of justice is too insignificant to receive God's notice and be rewarded:

---

[20] Matthew 25:31-36.

> Then the righteous will answer Him, 'Lord, when did we see You hungry, and feed You, or thirsty, and give You something to drink... a stranger, and invite You in, or naked, and clothe You... sick, or in prison, and come to You?' The King will answer and say to them, 'Truly I say to you, to the extent that you did it to one of these brothers of Mine, even the least of them, you did it to Me.[21]'

But neither is any neglect of the responsibility to regard those in need of justice excused:

> Then He will also say to those on His left, 'Depart from Me, accursed ones, into the eternal fire which has been prepared for the devil and his angels; for I was hungry, and you gave Me nothing to eat; I was thirsty, and you gave Me nothing to drink; I was a stranger, and you did not invite Me in; naked, and you did not clothe Me; sick, and in prison, and you did not visit Me.' Then they themselves also will answer, 'Lord, when did we see You hungry, or thirsty, or a stranger, or naked, or sick, or in prison, and did not take care of You?' Then He will answer them, 'Truly I say to you, to the extent that you did not do it to one of the least of these, you did not do it to Me.'[22]

In one parable, Jesus speaks of the rich man who is resigned to hell for continuously ignoring the poor, hungry beggar, Lazarus, who sat outside his gate, covered with sores.

---

[21] Matthew 25:37-40.
[22] Matthew 25:41-45.

He was close enough for the rich man to see, yet far enough away that he could be disregarded. The rich man did not loathe him as a nuisance; he simply negated him as a fellow human who deserved consideration. To him, the beggar was a non-being whose situation could be overlooked. As a member of the Jewish community, it wasn't that the rich man did not know better. He simply did not "listen to Moses and the prophets."[23]

Jesus' actions demonstrated concern for the marginalized. He invited sinners and outcasts to dine at his table and openly accepted their invitations. His ministry to women of various cultures, including the Samaritan woman at the well, the Syrophoenician woman, and the woman caught in adultery, as well as his close friendship with Mary and Martha, crossed boundaries and raised their status within his society.

He reserved his harshest rebuke for those Pharisees who feign religious piety while chiding him for ceremonial uncleanness,

> ... you ... clean the outside of the cup and of the dish; but your inside is full of greed and wickedness.[24]

> ... you pay tithes of mint, rue, and every kind of garden herb, and yet you ignore justice and the love of God; but these are the things you should have done without neglecting the others.[25]

To a lawyer standing by who was insulted by this rebuke, Jesus countered,

---

[23] Luke 16:19-31.
[24] Luke 11:39.
[25] Luke 11:42.

> *...[w]oe to you lawyers as well! For you load people with burdens that are hard to bear, while you yourselves will not even touch the burdens with one of your fingers.*[26]

Many Lukan parables infer justice themes. These include the parable of the Good Samaritan,[27] of the Rich Fool,[28] of the Prodigal Son,[29] of the Dishonest Manager,[30] of the Widow and Unjust Judge,[31] and of the Pharisee and the Tax Collector.[32]

While some political systems are, obviously, more unjust than others, Jesus was apolitical. He did not endorse any specific political structure. Though, indeed, He would not have upheld despotic, totalitarian, or repressive social, economic, or political regimes, He was not democratic or republican, socialist or capitalist. Nor did He champion either monarchial or democratic forms of government. He waved no flag for any kingdom but understood the profound reality that all humanly devised systems are flawed in some way and, therefore, subject to correction. No governmental system or mechanism for administrating justice was handed down from heaven.

Because of the Fall, we cannot fool ourselves that any attempt to set up a theocracy will be devoid of serious error. All our theology—our way of thinking about an infinite God—is framed in our finite mind. There can, therefore, never be a utopian theocracy or a theocratic utopia. No matter how thorough and deliberate our consideration, some aspects of the human challenge will be overlooked. For human beings

---

[26] Luke 11:49.
[27] Luke 10:25–37.
[28] Luke 12:13–21.
[29] Luke 15:11–32.
[30] Luke 15:11–32.
[31] Luke 18:1–8.
[32] Luke 18:9–14.

are limited in their ability to discern the degree of our fallenness and how it distorts our thinking and actions.

God intended that ancient Israel would operate as a theocracy that recognized God as the ruler whose chosen agents—the priests and prophet—exercised authority. These leaders were assumed to be under God's direct authority and faithfully ruling the community in observance of God's commandments and laws. Yet, as Scripture reveals, their attempts always fell short.

In modern times, John Calvin envisioned Geneva, Switzerland as a biblical theocracy: a city controlled by the clergy in which the Church, as God's representative, dominated all aspects of life. What resulted, instead, was a coerced external righteousness in which clergy determined what it meant to be a faithful Christian and punished infractions with arrest and even torture. This system did not pay attention to the fact that members of the clergy (including Calvin) who determined God's standard were themselves subject to human failure.[33]

Vatican City is the only society with an absolute theocratic monarchy ostensibly guided by Christian principles. As the supreme power, the Pope leads its executive, legislative, and judicial branches of government. Yet, a history of treachery, scandal, and abuses in the Catholic Church reveals the fallacy of believing any humanly devised government can be utopian. The Church's history also exemplifies how injustice can be woven into the fabric of culture as religious intolerance, misogyny, child abuse, and

---

[33] William Manchester. *A World Lit Only by Fire: The Medieval Mind and the Renaissance: Portrait of an Age.* New York: Little, Brown and Co, 1993, 190-191.

favoritism toward the rich and exploitation of the poor become part and parcel of the kingdom[34]

In the New World that came to be known as America, the theocracy established by Puritans made no room for the expression of freedom of religion, speech, or the press. In their attempt to rid the church and society of practices associated with Catholicism, they created new forms of intolerance. Government deputized clergy exerted enormous political influence; only church members could vote in political elections, so only someone certified as "godly" could hope to gain elected office. [35]

In either case, it was believed that an autocracy based entirely on biblical principles would yield a perfect habitation for all citizens. But, such an assessment did not take human fallenness into account, and these ventures failed to consider some complex issues. We should expect each of these systems to be flawed, exhibiting abuses of rigid adherence to humanly designed sanctions. To think otherwise would be idolatrous for several reasons. First, such thinking does not take seriously the reality that often within a, supposed, theocracy the rules have more to do with personal standards of piety than justice. Within any humanly engineered theocracy, we must question who sets the standards of what is right? Who decides the criteria or interprets what is godly and biblical behavior and what is not? Again, since we all suffer the moral frailty occasioned by the Fall, any assertion of unbiased application of these measures of justice is flawed.

Further, it is impossible to legislate morality or justice; since these begin, at their core, as inward dispositions and

---

[34] See James Hitchcock, *History of the Catholic Church: From the Apostolic Age to the Third Millennium*. San Francisco, CA: Ignatius Press, 2012.

[35] See Milan Zafirovski, *The Protestant Ethic and the Spirit of Authoritarianism: Puritanism, Democracy, and Society*. New York: Springer, 2007.

attitudes. And while Scripture advises us that we can only speak [and do] what is already deeply rooted in our heart,[36] the most we can do is constrain the negative personal and public outworking of unjust attitudes. Yet, as a feature of new creatureliness, we expect Christians to have a change of heart that renders them more just and a disposition displayed in more openness to justice.

During his earthly tenure, Jesus did not attempt to establish a theocracy. Instead, He interacted with the various groups within his society—the Essenes, the Pharisees, the Sadducees, and Zealots, and each had its own agenda. The Essenes eschewed public life, shunned Temple worship, and lived secluded, ascetic lives of manual labor. The Pharisees and Sadducees were the wealthier elements of the population—the high priests, aristocratic families, and merchants. They came under the influence of Hellenism, tended to have good relations with the Roman rulers of Palestine, and generally represented the conservative element within Judaism. Finally, the Zealots sought to incite the Jews to rebel against the Roman Empire and expel it from the Holy Land by force of arms.[37]

However, Jesus aligned himself with none of these groups. His message identified the true enemy of Israel not as Rome but as sin and Satan. What Jesus called for is the just treatment of every individual, no matter what the system. For him, allegiance to political systems, including one's nation-state, ethnic community, or class, took second place to allegiance to ushering in the claims of the Kingdom. In the Kingdom, love of neighbor, whether across the street or the

---

[36] Luke 6:45.

[37] See Anthony J. Saldarini, *Pharisees, Scribes and Sadducees in Palestinian Society: A Sociological Approach*. Grand Rapids, MI: Wm. B. Eerdmans Publishing Co. 2001.

globe, would be the rule. Jesus' assertion that "the poor you will always have with you"[38] does not endorse the situation where one-fourth of the world's population lives a comfortable or extravagant lifestyle at the expense of the majority of others who live in abject poverty or at a mere subsistence level. Nor was it license for members of Christ's body who enjoy 'the favor or blessing of God' to ignore the needs of masses who live lives of quiet–or loud–desperation. Nor was it an exoneration of the political and social systems underlying such desperation.

To say that Jesus was apolitical and endorsed no governmental system does not mean He did not recognize the inherent sinfulness of certain systemic actions that deprive individuals or entire classes of people of the dignity required for authentically human existence. Rather, Jesus described a continuing reality among fallen, unredeemed men and women who He knew would be prone to pursue individual personal gain at the expense of the wholeness of entire communities. He knew that, because of this fallenness, some individuals would pursue paths leading not only to their own impoverishment, but also to that of generations of their progeny. He was aware that the causes of such dehumanizing conditions would be both individual and personal, as well as corporate and communal.

Just as Israel's closeness to God was as much for service as for individual and communal blessing, the promise of God's provision for the faithful is not an endorsement of an individual's—or nation's—right to fare sumptuously as the rest of the world virtually goes to living hell. Relatedly, our "closeness" as Spirit-endowed believers is no vehicle for material aggrandizement and ego self-stimulation, while others are locked out of opportunities for genuine wholeness.

---

[38] Mark 14:7.

The blessing of God is not an invitation to "name and claim" an ever-increasing slice of the economic pie while the rest of the world fights over the crumbs that fall from the feast table. Instead, our spirit-empowerment and intellectual acuity are gifts to the church to assist it to work toward a more just future for all humankind—in this present world.

We cannot raise a utopian hope of ushering in the reign of Christ over a fully actualized Kingdom where righteousness and justice will be the order of the day and injustice will be banished forever. Yet, we are called to use our spiritual and intellectual gifts to assist the church in modeling the already–but not yet reality that the Holy Spirit makes possible in lives lived in authentic obedience to the dictate to work for justice.

The episode of Jesus with the Samaritan woman invites us to look at ethnic exclusion as a matter of injustice. His obedience to the Spirit's prompting that yielded a felt a necessity to go through the detested region of Samaria[39] speaks of God's acceptance of those we would reject. Further, it speaks of God's desire for reconciliation with and between all who are created in God's image.

Jesus regularly placed the needs of people ahead of religious piety. He touched those considered ceremonially unclean and untouchable. He healed on the Sabbath, and esteemed women at a higher level than society would allow, speaking to them as equal members of the community and insisting that they have the same right to fair treatment as men.[40]

The Early Church

After Jesus' death and ascension, the day of Pentecost can be interpreted as a liberative event. The Spirit's descent on

---

[39] John 4:7-30.
[40] John 5:8-16. 9:14-16.

those gathered in the Upper Room spilled onto a community from the Jewish diaspora who had gathered in Jerusalem. He made himself available to both genders and people of all races, cultures, disparate classes and regions, reverberating the declaration of Joel that *'everyone who calls on the name of the Lord will be saved.* [41]

The young church exemplified a bent toward justice in the at the believers *"... had all things in common; and... began selling their property and possessions and... sharing them with all, as anyone might have need.*[42] Within this seemingly idyllic, yet short-lived setting we are told again that *"... there was not a needy person among them, for all the* [property owners] *would sell* [their holdings] *and bring the proceeds of the sales.*[43] But soon, this multi-ethnic, multi-cultural congregation began to experience disparity as *"a complaint arose on the part of the Hellenistic Jews against the native Hebrews because their widows were being overlooked in the daily serving of food."*[44] Rather than ignore the problem, the apostles, set up a mechanism to address it.[45]

The Apostle Paul, the most prolific New Testament writer, is often criticized or dismissed by more progressive Christians as showing little concern for the social situation of his time. Admittedly, the issue was not Paul's central project. Rather, he wanted to ensure a solid foundation for the infant church within a politically and religiously hostile society. Yet, well-meaning, Christians have often used Paul's words to support all manner of injustice including slavery, sexism, and gender inequity in the home, society, and church, as well as the mistreatment of those who define themselves as part of the LGBQT community. Yet, Paul never meant it to be so. For

---

[41] Acts 2:21.
[42] Acts 2:44-45.
[43] Acts 4:34.
[44] Acts 6:1.
[45] Acts 6:2-3.

in his writings, we glimpse his coming to terms with justice issues as he struggled to place the infant Church on firm footing.

To insinuate that Paul had a narrowly defined agenda is to miss the full scope of his ministry. As the chief messenger to the Gentiles, however, Paul exemplified the justice of inclusion, extending the vision of God's Kingdom beyond the narrow confines of his strict Jewish community. He led a delegation that spoke on behalf of non-Jewish converts being exempt from the burden of Mosaic law. We first see this in his plea for the equitable treatment of gentile Christians by Jewish believers when he declares that, in Christ,

> "there is no distinction between Greek and Jew, circumcised and uncircumcised, barbarian, Scythian, slave and freeman[46]

And he reiterates again his assertion of inclusion within his culturally segregated environment in a statemen often mouthed by Christians that

> [t]here is neither Jew nor Greek.... slave nor free,... male nor female[47]

Yet, it is easy to over-spiritualize his declaration as relating only to a person's spiritual standing, insisting that it tells us nothing about how we should relates in everyday interactions with others. While some more conservative Christians might unwillingly concede a broader application than just the spiritual may be possible, they are often quick to assert that Paul limited his concern with how believers should

---

[46] Colossians 3:11.
[47] Galatians 3:28.

relate to each other. However, the attitudes and behaviors Paul was encouraging are foundational for how Christians should relate to the rest of the human community. As we see, Paul refused to hold up Jewish tradition as a standard for Gentile inclusion. Instead, he made it clear that they would not have to be circumcised or observe Mosaic Law, and they should not only be accepted as members—but equal members—of the Christian community. Furthermore, he held that even servants, such as Onesimus, should not only be treated humanely, but as brothers and sisters in faith once they had accepted Christ.[48]

In a highly patriarchal society and Christian community, his greetings to each church included women leaders by name, showing them the same respect as men.[49] He considered Apphia, Phoebe, Junia, Prisca, Euodia, and Syntyche, among other women, as co-workers in the Gospel. Despite later narrow renditions of Paul's attitude towards women's leadership, his mention of at least eighteen women in his letters indicates that he valued women for their work in the early church.

In the end, however, we cannot hold up Paul as our model for doing justice; that was not his mission. So, the question is not "what was Paul saying" or "what would Paul do?" Instead, we should be asking, "What *did* Jesus do?" We cannot use Paul's attempt to wrestle with the cultural difficulties of setting the infant church on solid footing as an excuse for escaping involvement in just causes.

The New Testament is replete with instances of the Spirit guiding believers to involve themselves in God's inclusive

---

[48] This assertion proved difficult for many white American slave-owners who struggled with the idea that they might be ethically obligated to free those black slaves who by accepting Christ had become their spiritual brother or sister.

[49] See, for example, Romans 16:1-16.

intentions, breaking down barriers that would have excluded some from fellowship based on some external distinction. For example, Phillip crossed racial lines to minister to the Ethiopian Eunuch, an African God-fearer.

Though he at first wrestled with inclusiveness, the apostle, Peter, crossed the cultural line by carrying the Gospel to the home of Cornelius, a Roman Centurion.[50] Yet he continued to wrestle with how to treat non-Jewish converts before being convinced by Paul that these should be accepted fully into the community.[51]

Peter also wrestled with how believers are expressly summoned to forego retribution or retaliation in favor of forgiveness and reconciliation and to leave issues of ultimate justice to God.[52] He finally had to concede that divine retribution may sometimes be activated providentially through human agents and political institutions.[53]

Another New Testament writer, James, took up Jesus' project of championing those who suffer oppression. He insists that the kind of the "religion that God… accepts as pure and faultless [involves]… look[ing] after orphans and widows in their distress."[54] James spoke to what he saw as unacceptable partiality in the assembly—church leaders favoring the rich and looking down on those less fortunate. He rebuked those who would pay more attention to, are more welcoming of, and provide more for those with means while allowing the poor to fend for themselves.[55] He later returns to and elaborates on the theme of justice in spelling out the futility of ill-gotten riches and the dire consequences for those

---

[50] Acts 10:1-11:18.
[51] Acts 11: 1-18.
[52] 1 Peter 2:21-23.
[53] 1 Peter 2:14.
[54] James 1:27.
[55] James 2:1-13.

who are unjust when, in the tradition of the prophets, he admonishes,

> *Come now, you rich, weep and howl for your miseries which are coming upon you. Your riches have rotted and your garments have become moth-eaten. Your gold and your silver have rusted; and their rust will be a witness against you and will consume your flesh like fire. It is in the last days that you have stored up your treasure!*[56]

Significantly, James was speaking to a carnal Church—Christians who were not Christlike—when he, again prophetically, reminds his hearers that God is not oblivious to injustice and that,

> *... the pay of the laborers who mowed your fields, and which has been withheld by you, cries out against you; and the outcry of those who did the harvesting has reached the ears of the Lord of Sabaoth. You have lived luxuriously on the earth and led a life of wanton pleasure; you have fattened your hearts in a day of slaughter. You have condemned and put to death the righteous man; he does not resist you.*[57]

Like the prophets, James does not scold the wealthy simply for being rich, but because their wealth was gained at the expense of those of whom they have taken advantage. Because they wanted to lead extravagant lifestyles, the wealthy have paid their workers less than fair wages and,

---

[56] James 5:1-3.
[57] James 5:1-6.

possibly, allowed them to work in unsafe or unhealthy working conditions.

Finally, at the close of Scripture, the Book of Revelation confirms that justice will be eternally established at the consummation of all things. Here we read that everyone at the Great White Throne will be judged "according to the works they have done."[58] Yet, depending on whether we read the book as conservative eschatology or progressive apocalyptic, we can come away with different views of the ultimate outworking of justice.

Within Conservative Christianity, John's vision is solely focused on a futuristic and final victory when, after a period of persecution for their faith, God rescues those who stand with God from all who stand against God. On the other hand, progressive readings find historical meaning and real-time implications for the issue of justice within its pages.

Yet, the book lends itself to a both/and rather than either/or interpretation. It begins by speaking to real people (the Seven Churches) about real persecution they were enduring at the hands of an actual political power (the Roman Empire) because of their faith.[59] This was a period where Christians experienced a variety of injustices: socially, they were ostracized by their communities; economically, they were deprived of their livelihood; and retributive injustice saw them wrongly imprisoned and killed. Yet, the book reveals a vision of a time when all oppression and injustice will end. Moreover, it calls to account those who would oppress God's people and promises that they will be recompensed for their injustice. Though the book depicts the battle as being dramatically and symbolically played out in

---

[58] Revelation 20:11-12.
[59] Revelation 2-3.

the earthly realm, the real struggle is on a higher plain, with the ultimate antagonism being between God and Satan.

Within this text, Scripture celebrates diversity, giving us a tantalizing glimpse of a glorious, multi-ethnic multitude praising God.

> *After these things I looked, and behold, a great multitude which no one could count, from every nation and all tribes and peoples and tongues, standing before the throne and before the Lamb, clothed in white robes, and palm branches were in their hands; and they cry out with a loud voice, saying,*
>
> *"Salvation to our God who sits on the throne, and to the Lamb."*[60]

Revelation speaks, again, of justice as an attribute of God's very nature and character:

> *And I saw as it were a sea of glass mingled with fire: and them that had gotten the victory over the beast, and over his image, and over his mark, and over the number of his name, stand on the sea of glass, having the harps of God. And they sing the song of Moses the servant of God, and the song of the Lamb, saying, Great and marvelous are thy works, Lord God Almighty; just and true are thy ways, thou King of saints."*[61]

In sum, biblical justice is social, economic, and political; it is concerned with the situations of those who inhabit the

---
[60] Revelation 7:9-10.
[61] Revelation 15:2-3.

mundane world that God so loved. The stranger, poor, widow, and others who are prey to any form of distress are the subjects of God's care and should be the focus of concern for those who identify as purveyors of God's kingdom.

Engaging biblical justice, then, involves an assumption that members of our families, faith community, local community, broader society, and world are interconnected. Hebrew Scripture embeds this in the concept of shalom—life lived with in an attitude of "all-rightness" with each other, the creator, and the environment in a world where all have the basics for flourishing and peace.[62] So, Christians who attempt to disentangle the Kingdom entirely from the messy world of earthly politics miss the point. They deprive our sacred text of its rightful claim to relevancy and spiritualize away the temporal value of applying its principles. Therefore, for Christians, justice is not an extracurricular or optional endeavor. It is not only for leaders or radical believers. Rather, this mandate as imperative for all believers, is rooted in Scripture and is the essence of who God is.[63]

Yet, Scripture reminds us that we should not expect the ultimate remedy of injustice to unfold until the full coming of the Kingdom. It is not that we should do nothing. Our daily lives should model what the kingdom will look like as we work to make individuals, communities, and the entire cosmos whole. For though Scripture withholds hope of doing away with injustice or destroying oppression before the second coming of Christ, we must never stand idly by as injustice unfolds. Instead, to name ourselves as Spirit-empowered, biblical Christians, we must own our call to stand against those who foster injustice and with those who are its victims.

---

[62] Howard Zehr, *The Little Book of Restorative Justice.* Intercourse, PA: Good Books, 2015, 17.

[63] Timothy Keller. *Generous Justice.* New York, NY: Riverhead Books, 2012.

5

Spirituality in Movements of Renewal

> "It will come about after this
> That I will pour out My Spirit on all mankind;
> And your sons and your daughters will prophesy,
> Your old men will have dreams,
> Your young men will see visions.
>
> Joel 2:28

The Azusa Street Revival that launched the contemporary renewal movement culminated several decades of the Holiness Movement's emphasis on the Holy Spirit's work in the life of the individual believer and the Church. It also reintroduced the Church to the vitality of the day of Pentecost, hearkening back to the Acts 2 depiction of the Upper Room in Jerusalem where the disciples gathered with other believers to await the fulfillment of Joel's prophesy and Jesus' promise. The attendees and other early Pentecostals sensed they were being empowered to usher in the kingdom of God in which Christ would be exalted over the principalities and powers of this world order and justice would reign. They saw the outpouring of the Holy Spirit in the biblical event of Pentecost as the former rain and their experience as the zenith of the Spirit's outpouring—the latter rain.

Participants viewed tongues speaking, first, as initial biblical evidence that God's Spirit had been poured out on them. But, they also saw it as a miraculous, xenolalic gift equipping them to evangelize the nations in their languages.

Several attempted, with different degrees of success, to put the gift to use in their missionary endeavors.

Reportedly, during her tenure in Liberia, Lucy Farrow used the Kru language to preach to people in their dialect. Also, reportedly, some to whom she ministered received the English language with their Holy Spirit baptism.[1] Alfred and Lillian Garr, reportedly, received the xenolalic gift of the language of India and Lillian believed she had been given the Tibetan and Mandarin dialects. When they attempted to use this gift in missionary efforts, however, they were disappointed and abandoned the insistence that tongues were a missionary tool.[2]

Early Pentecostals viewed physical, emotional, and mental healing as a sign of God's intervention as a convincing tool for winning the lost. Indeed they expected to replicate the miracles, signs, and wonders in the biblical narratives about Jesus, His disciples, and the apostles. Repeatedly, testimonies of miraculous healings were given at the revival, or poured in to editors of *The Apostolic Faith*, and were heard in congregations around the globe. The saints also expected and experienced deliverance from demonic activity and influences, and addictions of all types were regularly overcome.

At a time when the country was rigidly segregated by race and women were relegated to second-class citizenship, the revival projected an egalitarian, interracial ethos considered shocking by the broader Christian community and secular society. Revival leaders and participants not only talked about but actively modeled, racial, gender, and class inclusion. The congregation was multi-racial when such was largely unknown or outlawed throughout the country. Black,

---

[1] *The Apostolic Faith* 1:2 September 1907.
[2] Estrela Alexander, "Lillian Garr" in *The Women of Azusa Street*. Lanham, MD: Seymour Press, 2012, 86-98.

Latino, native, and Asian American men and women gathered with white Americans, Western and Eastern Europeans, and members of other ethnic groups in a run-down, former livery stable to worship the God of all humanity.

Class barriers were broken as seasoned ministers and denominational leaders stood, sat, or knelt beside common believers and received ministry from those to whom they would not have formerly extended a hand. At the revival, they treated each other with a deference that esteemed each man and woman regardless of race, class, social status, or ecclesial standing. No one was known by Reverend or Doctor or any other exalted "man-made" title, for these were considered unimportant. Instead, everyone, regardless of their ecclesial or social standing, was addressed as "brother" or "sister." Even Seymour was most often addressed in this manner.

Women's Equality

This radical egalitarianism opened access to women's full participation and leadership. It allowed them to use their natural talents and spiritual giftings to serve in positions that many outside the movement found scandalous: on the mission's administrative council, as respondents to the hundreds of correspondences that regularly deluged the mission. and as writers and editors for the monthly newspaper. They exhorted, prophesized, and preached to mixed audiences, laid hands on men and women to receive the baptism of the Holy Spirit and healing. Women led or were members of evangelistic teams that took the Pentecostal message to streets, tents, camp meetings, and churches around the Los Angeles area. They also led or joined missionary teams that took that message across the country and around the globe.[3]

Azusa Street believers sensed that God's Spirit had been poured out on "all flesh" for the "last days" endeavor of winning as many souls as possible. They supposed they were those who would prophesy to all nations to usher in the return of Christ and sensed an urgency for this task that prevented discrimination regarding which man or woman was called and qualified by the Spirit for this work. An element that drew particular public attention and derision from the secular press was the sight of prominent white clergy or community leaders kneeling before black women (who might have been their servants in more mundane circumstances) who prayed with them to receive Holy Spirit baptism.

Seymour insisted that the Bible supported women's equal involvement in God's work. Perhaps, one of the greatest evidences of his prophetic understanding of their role within the fledgling movement is reflected in his declaration that,

> Before Jesus ascended to heaven, holy anointing oil had never been poured on a woman's head; but before He organized His church, He called them all into the upper room, both men and women, and anointed them with the oil of the Holy Ghost, thus qualifying them *all* to minister in this Gospel. On the day of Pentecost, they *all* preached through the power

---

[3] For a broader overview of women's role and involvement in the revival see Estrelda Alexander, *The Women of Azusa Street*. (Lanham, MD: Seymour Press, 2019.

of the Holy Ghost. In Christ Jesus there is neither male nor female, all are one.[4]

Yet, as westernized Pentecostalism sought to gain respectability, it yielded some of its spiritual authority as the price of admittance into the broader evangelical community. One value it felt pressured to abandon was openness to women's leadership. So in this aspect, it grew to resemble its mainline and Evangelical brethren.

Even where women were no longer allowed official positions of authority, Pentecostal worship provided them unprecedented opportunities to exercise spiritual authority. They regularly exhorted, gave messages in tongues, or interpreted such messages. They acted as altar workers, praying with seekers for conversion, healing, deliverance, and Holy Spirit baptism. Within the congregation, as church mothers, older women set the spiritual tone, guided younger women, and advised the pastor.

As new Pentecostal congregations sprang up, many continued to make room for women's full participation. Where that did not happen, however, emboldened, Spirit-filled women established congregations in which they could freely exercise their gifts and encourage other women to move beyond the narrow bounds society and the church had established for them. Congregations established by Florence Crawford in Portland, Oregon, Mary Magdalena Tate in New Jersey, Aimee Semple McPherson in Los Angeles, Ida Robinson in Philadelphia, Rosa Horn in Harlem, and Mattie Thornton in Chicago eventually grew into viable, if not always sizeable, denominations.

---

[4]Untitled Article *Apostolic Faith*1:10 (Dec 1907), 4.

Racial Equality

The racial openness that was part of the spiritual ethos of early Pentecostalism came about as believers of various ethnicities understood themselves as well as their "other" brothers and sister as equally empowered by the Holy Spirit to be enlisted and fruitful in God's work. Many of the earliest renewal iterations were interracial. Repeated tributes to the Holy Spirit's power to break down racial barriers were included in testimonies and correspondences that flowed between the various revival sites.

This openness was part of the movement's Radical Holiness heritage that offered a criticism of racism that extended beyond the church to the American society.[5] The degree of racial harmony experienced at Azusa Street led Frank Bartleman to report in his later memoirs that "the color line was washed away in the blood [of Jesus]"[6] Another characterization put it more explicitly:

> It was something very extraordinary...white pastors from the South were eagerly prepared to go to Los Angeles to Negroes (sic), to fellowship with them and to receive through their prayers and intercessions the blessings of the Spirit. And it was still more wonderful that these white pastors went back to the South and reported that they had been together with

---

[5] In 1901, for example, one of its leaders, William Sched, published, *Is the Negro a Beast* with the Gospel Trumpet Publishing Company of Moundville, West Virginia to counter racist claims made in Charles Carroll's widely circulated, *The Negro a Beast* published that same year by the American Book and Bible House of St. Louis, Missouri:

[6] Frank Bartleman, *Azusa Street*. Plainfield, NJ: Logos International, 1980, 54.

Negroes (sic), that they had prayed in one Spirit and received the same blessing...[7]

Even at Azusa Street, however, the racial distinction was never entirely put aside. Some white leaders such as G.B. Cashwell struggled with its racial openness and exhibited some of the same concerns about blacks as many of his white Southern brethren.[8] Further, though several early groups attempted to maintain racial unity some of the movement's earliest divisions were along racial lines. Though the Pentecostal Assemblies of the World, the Church of God in Christ, the Fire Baptized Holiness Church, and other bodies began as racially inclusiveness organizations, within a few decades, a continually decreasing proportion maintained this commitment.

Self-Understanding

In the last quarter century, renewal spirituality has become the fastest-growing segment of the Christian community. Approximately 600 million Christians identify themselves as Pentecostal, Charismatic, and Neo-Pentecostal. Much of this growth has occurred in the two-thirds world, the segment of the global population most challenged by economic disparity and oppressive political systems. These renewal Christians share an openness to the

---

[7] Walter Hollenweger, *The Pentecostals: The Charismatic Movement in the Churches.* Minneapolis: Augsburg Press, 1972, 24.

[8] Though drawn to the Revival by reports of the Spirit's outpouring, Cashwell was disquieted by the thought of sitting under a black man's ministry and having blacks lay hands on him to pray for Holy Spirit baptism. Vinson Synan asserts, however, that after five days of seeking, he discarded racial feelings and invited Seymour and several others to lay hands on him, so that finally in late 1906, he received the Pentecostal experience. See Vinson Synan, *Oldtime Power: A Centennial History of the International Pentecostal Holiness Church.* Franklin Springs, GA: Lifesprings,107-108.

immediate engagement of the Holy Spirit as a central focus of their spirituality.

Yet, some outside the tradition negatively characterize it as, largely, attracting "disinherited,"[9] marginalized individuals who resort to religious fervor to mask social dislocation and lack of access to political and economic privilege. Such assessments place adherents in the "otherworldly" category of those who pay little attention to the social realities surrounding them in this world, and who routinely use ecstatic worship as a means of liminal escape to a better one. They see Pentecostalism, in particular, as a largely oral tradition, with no systematic laying out of its theological self-understanding.

How renewalists act, and what they do within the faith community, reflects their belief system—their theology. Everything renewalists do reveals a lived theology that fuses the sacred and secular around an understanding of a dynamic relationship with God. Every segment of renewalists' life is infused with, a lived pneumatology that sees the Holy Spirit as involved in the mundane, secular arenas of the believers' life as much as in sacred, spiritual elements.

Appreciating the breadth of renewalist pneumatology— the understanding, of the work and role of the Holy Spirit in the community—requires a variety of lenses. Within the multifaceted reality that has historically come to be known as the renewal movement, segments share distinctive yet integrally related expressions of spirituality. Indeed, what is perhaps most distinctive about this tradition is the variety in

---

[9] For example Robert Mapes Anderson titles his widely read historical accounting of the Pentecostal movement, published in 1979 by Oxford University Press *as, Vision of the Disinherited: The Making of American Pentecostalism.*

its spiritual expression. Whether in storefront edifices on metropolitan boulevards and side streets, expansive suburban megachurches, or moderate rural structures the Holy Spirit's dynamic presence is welcomed.

Renewal congregations are no longer solely relegated to the poor and dispossessed, though they have a higher representation among these groups. Unlike the first generations, later renewalists represent a range of socioeconomic and educational attainment. Leaders range from high-school-educated pastors who, convinced of their call and asserting they need nothing more than the Scripture and Holy Spirit anointing, to graduates of some of the most prestigious seminaries in the country. Again, what these individuals and groups share is an understanding that the Holy Spirit is personally accessible to the individual believer with a measure of empowerment and heightened spirituality. They still expect to experience the Spirit's expressed presence in the community's life and worship. So, while it may be easier to lump renewalists into a generic subculture, such a classification is an oversimplification

More than the measure of the Holy Spirit that all believers are understood to receive at regeneration, renewalists seek a biblical answer to the query, "Did you receive the Holy Spirit when you believed?"[10] They insist that the answer involves opening oneself to the full measure of power received through a baptism that renders the individual able to live a holy life. For, they maintain that this lifestyle is only achievable through the fullness of the Spirit. This is not to suggest that the Spirit-filled believer is impervious to sin. Rather, he or she is held to be supernaturally empowered to forcefully resist and overcome such temptation.

---

[10] Acts 19:2.

Holiness predecessors held Spirit baptism was witnessed by an undeniable inner deep peace and euphoric joy, and outward love of one's fellow person and a strong bent toward justice. Classical, Pentecostal spirituality added additional evidence of the initial physical sign of speaking in tongues. They contend that only the fully empowered believer can operate in the full measure of power and that through this experience, believers are enabled to accomplish "greater [supernatural] works:" divine healing, exorcism, deliverance, and to have supernatural faith to believe for other divine interventions.

Rooted in the Holiness movement's emphasis on personal and social ethics, the renewalist does not seek an experience simply as an indication of spiritual superiority. The impartation of the Spirit is expected to bring an ethical change. Indeed, one will be able to "live right" because, according to the saints, "you can't live right without the [baptism of the] Holy Ghost." Believers insist this baptism brings the supernatural ability to resist sin. An individual on whom the Holy Spirit has been poured out is expected to live and act perceivably different for as the popular chorus suggests, "I looked at my hands, my hands looked new; I looked at my feet and they did too." In other words, there should be a change in one's moral character.

The Spirit in the Community's Life

The discernible manifestation of the Holy Spirit is expected, invoked, and welcomed in every facet of the worship of the Spirit-empowered believer. The Spirit's presence is imparted through laying on of hands to minister spiritual, emotional, or physical healing, to consecrate leaders for ministry, or to minister deliverance from a variety of bondages. The Spirit speaks through testimony, the preached word, spoken or sung messages in natural language or tongues, interpretation of those messages, and prophetic pronouncement.

Renewalists contend that Spirit baptism brings a catalog of charismata or spiritual gifts—interpretation of tongues, word of knowledge, word of wisdom, discerning of spirits, prophecy, faith, healing, and working of miracles.[11] Though they reject cessationists' insistence that these gifts were relegated to the birth of the Church, renewalists often relegate the operation of these gifts to corporate worship or personal ministry.

"Interpretation of tongues" is understood as the supernatural ability to understand unlearned spiritual language and communicate what the Spirit intends to be heard. The "word of knowledge" involves revelation from God regarding situations about which the individual has no foreknowledge. The "word of wisdom" is the ability to appropriately apply existing knowledge. A person gifted to discern spirits can determine the underlying transcendent source and nature of encounters. While every Christian believer has a measure of faith, renewalists hold that the gift of supernatural faith positions the individual to believe for things considered beyond the bounds of everyday human experience. The gifts of healing are seen as the extraordinary ability to bring about physical, mental, or emotional healing without dependence on conventional medicine, and the working of miracles involves facilitating divine intervention in regular human affairs. The gift of prophecy is not simply foretelling, but forth-telling God's mind within

---

[11] See 1 Corinthians 12:8–10.

the sermon or exhortation, as part of a testimony, or as an extemporaneous address prompted by the Holy Spirit.

Most of Jesus' healing took place outside the temple. He healed the Syrophoenician woman and blind Bartimaeus on the road. He spoke the word of knowledge to the Samaritan woman at the well. Yet too often, among renewalists, the operation of the gifts has been limited to church worship. Historically, Classical Pentecostals have understood these gifts as working principally for edifying members of the faith community or evangelistically to bring people into the community. The 1960s Charismatic movement broadened classical Pentecostals' understanding of the Holy Spirit's role. Since many Charismatics had an appreciation for a social witness, ecumenical encounters moved the emphasis from glossolalia and allowed Pentecostal and Neo-Pentecostal and Charismatic camps to work closely on issues of justice.[12] The movement's communal nature promotes a progressive spirituality and a more holistic understanding that any gift residing within an individual or community must benefit the entire community. The liberative motif of Jesus' assertion that "the Spirit of the Lord is on me" resonated with believers who see Holy Spirit empowerment as the source for their urgency to bring good news to the poor and who work to set free those who are spiritually captive.

While some observers, such as ethicist, J Deotis Roberts, contend that the Pentecostal movement has been "notoriously short on social conscience and social justice"

---

[12] Kilian McDonnell, *Toward a New Pentecost.* Collegeville, MN: The Liturgical Press, 1974, 50. For a concise, excellent synopsis of the Charismatic movement's contribution to ecumenical dialog see Leon Joseph Cardinal Suenens, *Ecumenism, and Charismatic Renewal*: Theological and Pastoral Orientations. London: Darton, Longman & Todd, 1978.

with "little concern for social transformation,"[13] renewalist congregations exhibit a full range of responses to justice depending, as in other traditions, on the prophetic vision of their leaders and the particular political proclivity and social consciousness of their membership. Some individuals and congregations have provided progressive practical approaches for the communities they serve, involving themselves in social action and benevolence. Innovative programs combine preaching of the gospel and ministry to spiritual, emotional, and material needs with advocacy, education, and social empowerment.[14] Other segments of the movement have maintained status quo, 'quasi-biblical', interpretations of contemporary problems such as race relations, urban violence, family and community disassociation, and gender issues without making any meaningful contributions.

Likewise, we can compare the theological maturity of various segments of the movement. Some primarily larger, more progressive congregations and denominations take the tasks of theological reflection and articulation seriously and have begun developing cohesive, systematic doctrinal statements and theological treatises regarding justice. This

---

[13] J. Deotis Roberts, *Black Theology in Dialogue.* Philadelphia: Westminster, 1987, 59.

[14] Herbert Daughtry's House of the Lord Pentecostal Church in Brooklyn, New York, Arthur Brazier's Apostolic Faith Church in Chicago, and Eugene Rivers' Azusa Community in Boston are excellent examples of this type of "Progressive Pentecostalism." See, for example, Sammie M. Dortch, *When God Calls: A Biography of Arthur M. Brazier.* Grand Rapids, MI: Wm. B. Eerdmans Publishing Co., 1996, Herbert D. Daughtry, Sr., *No Monopoly on Suffering: Blacks and Jews in Crown Heights (And Elsewhere).* New York: Africa World Press, 1997, and Wendy Murray Zoba, " Separate and Equal - Martin Luther King Dreamed of an Integrated Society—Boston Minister Eugene Rivers Thinks it was the Wrong Dream" *Christianity Today,* August 1, 2001. https://www.christianitytoday.com/ct/2001/augustweb-only/8-6-24.0.html

group has broken rank with their peers by refuting biblical literalism and reconsidering the nature of biblical authority. At the same time, they attempt to respond to contemporary issues such as racism, gender equity, poverty and economic injustice, homosexuality, and HIV/AIDS with more compassionate and nuanced strategies.

Other segments of the movement maintain an essentially oral and eclectic theological tradition that eschews the contemporary situation. They see the tendencies of more progressive siblings as spiritual compromise and a threat to the movement's integrity and unity. For them, such compromise stifles the opportunity for dynamic revelation by the Holy Spirit and is synonymous with retreat. They maintain their historical disdain for "man-made" theologies, often preferring to see the Bible as their only frame of reference. With that measure of empowerment we have received, renewalists must attempt to faithfully answer questions that challenge individual flourishing. These are a starting point for developing a compassionate, yet systematic, theological stance that addresses justice issues in the world in which we are—willingly or not—a part. Importantly, this theology must retain our distinctive ethos while addressing biblical and contextual mandates for individual, communal and global justice while reflecting a self-understanding of openness to God's Spirit for individual and communal revelation and empowerment to act on God's behalf as we mediate concern for the world God so loves.

6

So Great a Cloud of Witnesses

Therefore, since we have so great a cloud of witnesses surrounding us, let us also lay aside every encumbrance and the sin which so easily entangles us, and let us run with endurance the race that is set before us[1]

Granted, criticism of the modern renewal movement as essentially a "Spirit" or "tongues" sect with no cohesive theological foundation and a preoccupation with otherworldly sensibilities and personal piety to the neglect of the social realities is, somewhat, justified. Moreover, contentions by some scholars that one rarely finds activist strands within the movements, or leaders who regularly address community issues or even grave injustice from their pulpits is founded. Further, sermons seldom address current social themes.[2]

However, a closer look at the movement's diverse history questions whether this reputation is, entirely, deserved. In any diverse movement, there are a variety of responses regarding very important issue. Still, a minority of, progressive renewalists have historically offered practical approaches for their communities, even while other have maintained status quo, 'quasi-biblical' interpretations that provided no substantive contribution to conversations regarding justice.

---

[1] Hebrews 12:1.
[2] Except to reflect some specific sin such as high rates of teen pregnancy, or extra-marital sexual involvement, or what is perceived as the gay "agenda," especially unless an issue directly affects the immediate community. This distancing is often true, however, on issues as closely tied to doctrinal beliefs as anti-abortion and right-to-life sentiments.

On its face, Amos Yong's assertion that much of classical Pentecostalism has had a "typical apolitical orientation"[3] misses an important truth. For no theology has a genuinely a-political orientation. All theology has the pragmatic goal of preserving or dismantling a social reality that is presumed to be God-ordained or against the will of God. Granted, to borrow a comparison used by Howard W. Stone and James Duke in their important volume, *How to Think Theologically*, within the Holiness-Pentecostal–Charismatic continuum, that political orientation has been more embedded than deliberate. In their work, the writers challenge Christians to examine inherited ways of thinking about central issues of faith, and wrestle with this thinking to come to well thought-out convictions rather than simply clone the understandings of others.[4]

When we authentically do this, we come to see any theology that provides a foundation for sanctioning bigotry or injustice or that provides a base for disengagement from the work of justice seeking as unscriptural and unsound. We understand that any theological system that props up structures of oppression is inauthentic in its claim to be biblical. Any theological system that does not take seriously the liberative work of the Holy Spirit and the implications of Jesus assertion that, "I have come that you might have life, more abundantly" is inauthentic. Any theology that does not enter into Jesus' project of proclaiming and pushing forward the possibility of that abundant life within the already present

---

[3] Amos Yong, "Justice Deprived, Justice Demanded: Afropentecostalisms and the Task of World Pentecostal Theology Today," *Journal of Pentecostal Theology* 15:1 [2006], 130. Yong has otherwise advocated for Pentecostal engagement with the political, including, but not limited to, in his *In the Days of Caesar: Pentecostalism & Political Theology*. Grand Rapids, MI: Wm B. Eerdmans Publishers, 2010.

[4] Howard K. Stone and James O. Duke. *How to Think Theologically*, 2nd Edition. Minneapolis: Fortress Press, 2006.

manifestation of the kingdom, while being cognizant that its full presentation is only possible in the undetermined not yet, is impotent. Further, whenever an individual or group hides behind the Bible as an excuse to ignore the plight of the oppressed, they are not in line with Scripture' mandate for justice seeking.

As a political theologian, my contention that all theology is political suggests how we are shaped by our reality and this reality colors how we think about God and God's ordering of, and relationship to, the world. While renewalist theology is a lived theology springing from a rich heritage of lived pneumatology, among people of color, the poor, women, and other oppressed communities it has not always taken full advantage of what that pneumatology offers. Rather, it has allowed some to settled for liminal experiences that provide escape from the mundane or even threatening issues of everyday realities into moments of ecstasy. In that way it has been enough to keep them from losing their minds but not enough to empower them to deliver their communities from the surrounding evil of oppression and injustice.

Unfortunately, the lack of theological deliberateness regarding our politics and our lack of political deliberateness regarding our theology has rendered a portrait of classical Pentecostalism that resonates with Robert's contention of the lack of the movement's social conscience or concern for social transformation. Yet, progressive Pentecostals would insist that personal piety plays out in just relationships among the faithful and broader community. And, like Roberts, Iain MacRobert asserts, that the distinction between individual and social ethics disappears in the self-understanding of African American Pentecostals:

> The sacred and profane [are] totally integrated in the[ir] holistic world view... God [was] experienced in all of life, bringing power, liberty, joy, and solace... [T]he same Spirit which had been in Christ and in the Apostles [was] in them as they carried salvation and healing to the urban ghettoes.... Not only did the Spirit equip them to transform society—to obliterate the color line through the power of love—[The Spirit] also liberated them spiritually, psychologically, and socially, transforming poor, dispossessed, disenfranchised, ill-educated, powerless black people who were despised and constantly being told they were inferior by white society... [into] the children of God—the saints of the Most High![5]

While such critical assessments leave two divergent impressions of lack or inclusion of justice seeking within the classical Pentecostal context, Roberts' an MacRobert's appraisals invite revisiting and re-appropriating the liberative witness of some early formulations to discover what renewal leaders have contributed to the arena. From inception, progressive renewalists were spurred as much by social and economic realities as a thirst for spiritual renewal of the church and nation. Indeed, some saw these two issues as intricately and inextricably intertwined.

Early Liberative Expressions

The Holiness Movement

Formal theological or Bible school training was rare among early Holiness and Pentecostal leaders who were

---

[5] Iain MacRobert, *The Black Roots and White Racism of Early Pentecostalism.* New York: Palgrave Macmillan; 1st ed. 1988, 90.

considered unlearned by other Christian traditions. Yet, these leaders understood, intuitively, that their social reality was inconsistent with the biblical witness. As Pentecostalism's forerunner, the Holiness Movement produced a cadre of men and women who took the temporal plight of their communities seriously. Many incorporated prophetic critiques of injustice into the ecclesial structures they created. Drawing on the authority of Spirit-inspired biblical interpretation for pronouncements and actions, radical Holiness leaders addressed race, gender, economic disparity, and war with the same vigor as the need for personal holiness.

On one early issue–abolition–numerous individuals, publications, and institutions supported a just stance. The editors of the *Guide to Holiness*, for example, were abolitionists.[6] In its nascent period, Oberlin College advocated "civil disobedience" against fugitive slave laws.[7] The founding of the institution was a high point for the egalitarian and racially inclusive Holiness movement.

Methodist Episcopal Church bishop and passionate reformer, Gilbert Haven, was the second president of the church's Freedman's Aid Society. Haven not only took on abolitionist and feminist causes, but advocated interracial marriage.[8] LaRoy Sunderland, a founder of Houghton College, withdrew from the Methodist Episcopal Church in 1840 after being defrocked for his anti-slavery writings. Sunderland helped found the explicitly abolitionist, Wesleyan Methodist Church and was a founding member of William Lloyd Garrison's American Anti-Slavery Society. Yet, he ended his life as an atheist partly because of the

---

[6] The *Guide was* the chief periodical of the perfectionist movement.

[7] Leading to the Oberlin-Wellington Rescue Case—an important event in the history of American civil liberties.

[8] William Gravely, *Gilbert Haven, Methodist Abolitionist: A Study in Race, Religion, and Reform, 1850-1880*. Nashville: Abingdon Press, 1973.

inconsistency he saw in the church's proclamation and its witness to justice.⁹ When the Missouri Conference of the Methodist Church voted to join the pro-slavery Methodist Episcopal Church South in 1845, Anthony Bewley, a white circuit rider and antislavery proponent, refused to accept this decision. And he remained in what he considered the true Methodist Church. While some northern Methodist abolitionists saw him as weak on the slavery issue, his fiery sermons enlisted people for the cause. Southerners accused him of being a John Brown sympathizer and slave agitator and lynched him.¹⁰ These radical Holiness proponents not only believed that slavery, racial inequality, and lack of empathy for the poor were inconsistent with the Gospel, they felt compelled to act.

Founded in 1881, fifteen years after slavery legally ended, the Evening Light Saints bore witness to the ideal of racial and gender equality. From its inception, this group (which became the Church of God (Anderson, Indiana)—or the Church of God Reformation Movement) has been among the most racially diverse Christian bodies in the United States. This legacy is primarily due to the theological commitment of its founder, Daniel S. Warner. From its earliest history, Warner's group welcomed blacks, and both black and racially mixed congregations were in existence as early as 1896. Further, the Saints provided a theological critique of racial prejudice, holding that interracial worship was a sign of the true Church. Instead of testifying that they were "saved, sanctified and

---

[9] For a discussion of Sunderland's career see Edward D. Jervey, "LaRoy Sunderland: Zion's Watchman" *Methodist History* 6:3 (April 1968), 16-32. For a discussion of his abolitionist activities, see Herman E. Thomas, "Abolition and the Wesleyan Methodist Connection in America" *AME Zion Quarterly Review* 111 (January 1999), 18-29.

[10] Charles Elliott, "Martyrdom of Bewley" *Methodist Review* 45 (October 1863), 626-645.

filled with the Holy Ghost," the Saints were likely to assert they were "saved, sanctified, and prejudice removed."[11] Blacks and whites sat together in their interracial services, and both ministered regularly. Warner and his followers abandoned hierarchical denominational structures to restore 'New Testament' unity among genders and races, even blatantly disregarding existing mores. Their flaunting of societal norms often drew open hostility from surrounding communities and proved personally dangerous for its members. Undeterred, their position appealed to blacks such as Azusa Street founder, William Joseph Seymour. Among the Saints, he found a place of complete acceptance and affirmation. The group licensed and ordained him as part of its army of itinerant tent-making evangelists. While with them, he encountered their communal homes where members supported each other's daily life and ministry, a pattern he later incorporated into the Azusa Street Mission.

When William Christian, late-nineteenth-century founder of the Church of the Living God (Christian Workers for Fellowship), aggressively addressed inequality and racist philosophies, he targeted claims of some white Baptists that blacks were non-human products of a human father and female beast. Conversely, he claimed that the biblical saints were black and grounded his anthropology in a reworked Christology that posited Jesus as a black descendant of Abraham and David's lineage.[12] In his denomination's catechism, Christian explicitly proclaimed the value of African spirituality while not demonizing other races. Its faith

---

[11] B. Scott Lewis, "William J. Seymour: Follower of the 'Evening Light'" *Wesleyan Theological Journal* 38:2 (2004),172.

[12] "A Catechism: The Church of the Living God," <www.mc.maricopa.edu/~kefir/club/african_ american/index.html>. See also Walter Hollenweger "Black Pentecostal Concept," *Concept* 30. Geneva, Switzerland: World Council of Churches, 1970, 16-19.

statement asserts that "[we] believe in the Fatherhood of God and the Brotherhood of man" and "...that all men are born free and equal."[13]

In his *Appeal to the Sons of Africa*, Charles Price Jones, co-founder of the Church of God in Christ and founder of the Church of Christ (Holiness) USA,[14] employed an essentially reformist approach to race issues. He implored blacks not to respond to white oppression with immoral or unethical behavior, but to uplift themselves and trust God for ultimate deliverance. Yet, his stance cannot be dismissed as totally otherworldly, since Jones was as concerned about the temporal welfare of blacks as about their eternal state. He was particularly concerned that they respect and honor each other in the face of dishonor from the white community.[15]

Evangelist and missionary, Amanda Berry Smith often addressed predominantly white audiences as both a temperance proponent and an outspoken critic of racial disparity. Smith used the language of sanctification synonymously with liberation. She insisted that "the blood of Jesus" not only freed her from personal sin but delivered her from an inadequate estimate of the divine worth of black people. Smith's autobiography critiqued sexism and racism in the church and society. At one point, she contended that "...some people would understand the quintessence of sanctifying grace if they could be black about twenty-four

---

[13] Ibid.

[14] See Anita Bingham Jefferson, *Charles Price Jones: First Black Holiness Reformer with a One Hundred Year Chronology of His Life*. Florence, MS: Stephens Printing, 2011.

[15] Charles Price Jones, *Appeals to the Sons of Africa: A Number of Poems, Readings, Orations and Lectures, Designed Especially to Inspire Youth of African Blood with Sentiments of Hope and Nobility as well as to Entertain and Instruct All Classes of Readers and Lovers of Humanity*. Jackson, MS: Truth Publishing Company, 1902.

hours."[16] After retiring from the mission field, she founded the Amanda Smith Orphanage and Industrial Home for Abandoned and Destitute Colored Children.

Those within the Holiness ranks understood the relationship between the personal and social aspects of the gospel–personal and social holiness–and sought to not only speak about but live out this radical vision. The heritage to the next generation of believers would set a foundation for Pentecostals who sought to follow the same path.

Early Pentecostalism

Birthed out of the ethos of its antecedent, early Pentecostalism continued the multiracial, egalitarian ethos. In its founding at the Azusa Street Revival, these elements made this unique spiritual event even more unusual within the surrounding racist, classist, and sexist society in which it unfolded. The revival's leader, Seymour, and many surrounding him understood the Holy Spirit outpouring on believers of every race and class as a vehicle for unifying a divided church and world. While segregation and patriarchy were the society's norms, this egalitarian ethos exhibited itself in women's prominent roles in every aspect of the Azusa Street mission and revival. It was also evidenced in their significant role in moving the Pentecostal message across the nation and world. The lack of class distinction among participants further expressed its egalitarian ethos as seasoned clergy worshipped alongside dedicated laypeople

---

[16] Amanda Berry Smith, *An Autobiography: The Story of the Lord's Dealings with Mrs. Amanda Smith, the Colored Evangelist: Containing an Account of Her Life Work of Faith, and Her Travels in America, England, Ireland, Scotland, India, and Africa as an Independent Missionary*. Chicago: Meyer & Brother Publishers, 1893. See also, Adrienne Israel, *Amanda Berry Smith: From Washerwoman to Evangelist*, Lanham, MD: Scarecrow Press, 1998.

and the newly converted. In addition, black washwomen and household servants regularly prayed with pastors and other dignitaries to receive the Pentecostal experiences of Holy Spirit baptism, healing, and deliverance.

Since Seymour saw what was unfolding before him as God's miraculous, unifying move, it devastated him that Charles Parham, among other white leaders, failed to perceive the moment's spiritual significance. Seymour insisted that a more sure sign of Holy Spirit baptism was love that resulted in undivided unity between believers of every sort.[17] Yet, after years of corporate revival and personal effort, he was broken-hearted when such unity did not become a reality.

Seymour's disappointment was shared by another who recognized the revival's prophetic potential: itinerant evangelist, revival participant, and armchair historian, Frank Bartleman. Before coming to Azusa Street, Bartleman was involved in several social outreach efforts, including Alma White's Pillar of Fire inner-city rescue mission in Denver, the Salvation Army, and Chicago's Gospel Mission.[18] Though contemporary renewalists often quote his hopeful, yet premature, assessment that "the color line was washed away in the blood," Bartleman spoke of the lost opportunity of the revival's potentially prophetic witness.[19]

After receiving divine healing from a debilitating injury, physician, Finis Yoakum, relinquished his practice to establish the Pisgah House mission. Through this ministry, started in 1895, he offered housing, medical care, food, and

---

[17] Seymour, William J. *Doctrines and Disciplines of the Apostolic Faith Mission of Los Angeles*, edited Larry Martin. Joplin, MO: Christian Life Books, 2000, 51-53.

[18] Frank Bartleman, *From Plow to Pulpit*. Los Angeles: Frank Bartleman, 1924, 32-33.

[19] Ibid., 8-79.

clothing, along with spiritual support to the homeless, alcoholics, drug addicts, prostitutes, and those who were simply indigent. By 1911, Yoakum had experienced Pentecostal Holy Spirit baptism, and the home and several sister locations provided housing for 173 people, 9,000 clean beds, and 18,000 meals monthly throughout Los Angeles.[20]

Charles Harrison Mason, founder of the Church of God in Christ,[21] modeled racial reconciliation,[22] adamantly insisted that black Christians acknowledge their African heritage, and took pains to provide biblical sanction for inclusion of this heritage within COGIC culture.[23] Though his sermons dealt primarily with eternal matters, Mason regularly addressed two temporal issues: pacifism and lynching. His outspoken pacifist convictions kept him under Federal Bureau of Investigation surveillance, leading to incarceration on at least two occasions. He vocalized his conviction that lynchings were carried out because preachers were "leading people away from the reproof of God and not to the glory of God [and that they were] cowards until they are baptized with Jesus' baptism."[24] He also received attention from federal law enforcement officials because of alliances with white

---

[20] Jennifer A. Stock, "Finis E. Yoakum, M.D. : Servant to the Disinherited of Los Angeles, 1895-1920. Paper presented at the 20th annual meeting of the Society for Pentecostal Studies, Christ for the Nations Institute, Dallas, Texas, November 8-10, 1990.

[21] The largest black Pentecostal body (and arguably the largest Pentecostal body) in the United States.

[22] Elijah L Hill. *The Missing Link of the American Civil Rights Movement: The Pre-Civil Rights Contribution of Bishop C.H. Mason*. S.l.: Createspace, 2016.

[23] Craig Scandrett-Leatherman, "The African Roots of the Church of God in Christ." Paper presented at the 31st annual meeting of the Society for Pentecostal Studies, Southeastern College, Lakeland, Florida, March 14-16, 2002.

[24] This quote is from a sermon Mason preached on Sunday at the Church of God in Christ Convocation, December 7, 1919. It raises a question of what cowardly preachers Mason was talking about—white or black, present or absent.

colleagues when such overtures drew suspicion. Like Seymour, Mason viewed the dismantling of racial prejudice as a work of the Spirit. More importantly, he attempted to live out that conviction within COGIC and the broader community.[25]

In 1946, his congregation hosted educator and civil rights activist, Mary McLeod Bethune.[26] Two years later, it was the site for a meeting of Paul Robeson's Interracial Progressive Party.[27] Then, in 1959, Mason offered his church site for a Freedom Rally for the Memphis Volunteer Ticket Campaign, and it became the de facto center of Memphis' growing anti-segregation efforts.[28]

Whether they had their founder's vision in mind is unknown. Yet several progressive COGIC leaders actively participated in the 1950s and 1960s civil rights activism. Among them Ithiel and Frank Clemmons, Frederick Washington in New York, James Oglethorpe Patterson in Memphis, and William Roberts and Louis Ford in Chicago would carry out this ethos through practical engagement. Further, several other progressive COGIC leaders openly participated in civil rights activities or worked behind the scenes.

Politically active, Washington established one of the largest Brooklyn, New York churches of any denomination at its time. Yet, his ministry bore its most visible fruit in mentoring the young civil rights activist, Alfred Charles (Al)

---

[25] See, for example, Elton Weaver, *Bishop Charles H. Mason in the Age of Jim Crow: The Struggle for Religious and Moral Uplift*. Lanham, MD: Lexington Books, 2020.

[26] Facilitated through her friendship with COGIC Women's Department leader, Lillian Brooks Coffey.

[27] Michael Honey, *Going Down Jericho Road: The Memphis Strike, Martin Luther King's Last Campaign*. New York: W. W. Norton & Company, 2008, 19.

[28] Burleigh Hines, "5,000 Bury Uncle Toms at Rally," *Tri-State Defender*, August 8, 1959, 1.

Sharpton Jr. He was ordained as a teenager and cut his preaching and political teeth in Washington's church. Yet, partly because of disappointment in the level of Pentecostal social engagement, the community organizer, politician, and public media figure would eventually leave the movement for the Baptist Church.[29]

The legacy of Ithiel and Joseph Clemmons demonstrates that renewal leaders could be simultaneously preachers, scholars, and activists. The highly educated brothers built vital congregations while seeking racial justice and forging ecumenical alliances within and outside the renewal community. For example, Ithiel's theology of reconciliation helped shape the so-called "Memphis Miracle," a conference of Pentecostals and Charismatics that replaced the almost all-white umbrella organization, the Pentecostal Fellowship of North America with the racially mixed body, the Pentecostal-Charismatic Churches of North America.[30] His younger brother, Joseph, was elected to the Connecticut House of Representatives for two terms, served on the board of directors of Norwalk Economic Opportunity Now (NEON), and founded Pivot Ministries, a Christ-centered drug program.[31]

In 1955, Louis Henry Ford eulogized Emmitt Till, the young teenager whose brutal murder at the hands of Mississippi racists was the catalyst for heightened civil rights activity throughout the country. Within his Chicago community and the nation, Ford was a strong advocate for

---

[29] Michael Klein, *Man Behind the Sound Bite: The Real Story of the Rev. Al Sharpton.* New York: Castillo International, 1991.

[30] Marlon Milner, "We've come this Far by Faith: Pentecostalism and political and Social Upward Mobility among African-Americans" *Cyberjournal for Pentecostal-Charismatic Research.* ///c|/cyberj9/millner2.htm[3/8/2013 8:34:36 am.

[31] Ibid.

social justice, including serving as co-chairmanship of the 1965 Chicago Conference to Fulfill These Rights Now. In addition, he co-convened Ministers United in the 1980s and fought homelessness and drug dependency at the national level.[32]

William Roberts served as treasurer of the Board of Education of the National Fraternal Council of Negro Churches. In 1941, before the Civil Rights Movement was in full swing, Roberts was a member of the delegation from the organization that went to Washington to demand economic justice in jobs and reparations for African Americans.[33]

After Mason's death, J.O. Patterson, the first elected COGIC Presiding Bishop, sought to remind black secular and Christian activists of the indispensability of spiritual empowerment for social struggle. Patterson marched alongside King in Memphis, fought structural racism through his involvement in the Civil Rights protest in the 1960s, and encouraged organizations like the NAACP, but later distanced himself and his denomination from what he saw as "radical" activists and Black Power rhetoric.[34]

Nearly twenty years after COGIC's founding, former Methodist, William T. Phillips established the Ethiopian Overcoming Holy Church of God, expressly to meet the spiritual needs of black people within the segregated American South. The organization's original name shows evidence of Phillips' pro-African sentiments. Though he changed the designation to the Apostolic Overcoming Holy

---

[32] Estrelda Alexander, "Ford, Louis. Henry. 1914–1995" in The Dictionary of Pan-African Pentecostalism, Volume One: North America. Eugene, OR: Wipf and Stock, 2018, 171-172.

[33] Estrelda Alexander, "Roberts, William" in Ibid., 350-351.

[34] Thom Finley, "A Church Where Jesus Is Real": Race, Religiosity and the Legacies of Protest Activism in the Church of God in Christ, 1968-1989." B. A. Thesis Brown University, 2014. https://www.brown.edu/ academics/ history/sites/academics-history/files/images/Finleythesis.014.cogic.pdf.

Church of God to reflect a more inclusive ecclesiology,[35] the denomination maintains its earlier commitment to meeting the needs of its mostly black constituency. While AOHC maintains an exclusivist posture toward other Christian groups (even other Pentecostals in spiritual matters), it has been willing to join them in promoting the practical benefit of the black community, and while not fellowshipping in worship, Phillips associated with secular leaders on justice issues. He was so active in supporting the Civil Rights struggle, for instance, that his home was bombed in 1965.[36]

After World War I, Elias Dempsey Smith, founder of Triumph the Church and Kingdom of God, became enamored with Ethiopianism, incorporating some elements of the philosophy into his ecclesiology.[37] Smith distinguished between the "church militant of whites and the peace-loving church of blacks" and urged his followers to stand against subtle prejudice and segregation in church and society, cautioning them, "[d]on't be looking for a white Jesus coming down on a cloud…" Today, the denomination carries Smith's afro-centric ecclesiology further, espousing an anthropology that teaches, for example, that,

> … in God's everlasting Kingdom, there is an original language that God gave man in the Garden of Eden when he created Adam and Eve… for… the Holy Ghost will teach a language that the kingdoms of this

---

[35] For a discussion of COGIC involvement in the Civil Rights Movement, see Jonathan Chism, *Saints in the Struggle: Church of God in Christ Activists in the Memphis Civil Rights Movement, 1954–1968*. Lanham MD: Lexington Books, 2021.

[36] See Juanita Roby Arrington, *A Brief History of the Apostolic Overcoming Holy Church of God, Inc., and Its Founder: Including "What We Believe."* Birmingham, AL: Forniss Print Company, 1984

[37] See discussion of Triumph the Church and Kingdom of God in Chapter 3, and of the Apostolic Overcoming Holy Church in Chapter 6 of this text.

world will not be able to learn unless they are filled with that Spirit.[38]

Further, it insists that,

God will return every earthly kingdom to the people that came from beyond the rivers of Ethiopia. Many nations and kingdoms all over the world have been built by the blood, sweat, and slavery of Ethiopian descendants. The DNA of Ethiopia is everywhere on this earth.... God has (en)trusted the Jews with a dispensation, and... the Gentiles with a dispensation, but God is now calling Ethiopia. God will turn every kingdom of this world over to us.[39]

As a young journalist for two African American newspapers in Indianapolis, Garfield T. Haywood's caricatures depicted racial discrimination in that community and the nation. Though not prolific, his writings show a commitment to maintaining inter-racialism amid the rampant racism of his time. As the first presiding bishop of the Pentecostal Assemblies of the World, Haywood, did not ignore the racial realities of his constituencies. Yet, as its head, he struggled to maintain its multiracial presence and existence as an integrated body in both Southern and Northern regions of the country as a testimony to lived protest against discrimination. Further, his Indianapolis

---

[38] "Church Covenant" Triumph the Church and Kingdom of God, Sixth Episcopal District. http://www.triumpthechurchnat.org/creed%20%Anthem.htm#Creed/Anthem

[39] Ibid.

congregation was interracial, even while the state maintained a heavy Ku Klux Klan presence.[40]

Another Oneness leader, Robert Clarence Lawson, founder of the Church of Our Lord Jesus Christ of the Apostolic Faith, was an entrepreneur and community activist who energetically supported civil rights. He began by establishing businesses to give access to services and uplift the economic status of those within his Harlem community. At the same time, he demonstrated that black people could not be constricted within segregated neighborhoods by establishing the African American enclave of Lawsonville in the white community in Shrub Oak, New York. In Southern Pines, North Carolina, he took over a boarding school that became known as the R.C. Lawson Institute and founded an orphanage. Further, he encouraged "theological" education by establishing the Church of Christ Bible Institute as the training center for his denomination.

Lawson worked with Senator Adam Clayton Powell, Jr. to push black voter registration and participated in the first March on Washington in 1957 to encourage the federal government to grant black people voting rights. While firmly holding to conservative theological moorings, Lawson was a fervent Pan-Africanist. In 1958, he joined Nation of Islam leader, Malcolm X, at the first Africa Freedom Day[41] observance and the Conference of Independent African States held an evening rally at his Harlem congregation, Refuge Temple. As president of the Ethiopian World Federation, he visited that country, received the Star of Ethiopia from his

---

[40] See Talmadge French, *Early Interracial Oneness Pentecostalism: G. T. Haywood and the Pentecostal Assemblies of the World (1901-1931)*. Eugene, OR: Pickwick Publications, 2014.

[41] Later known as African Liberation Day.

friend, Emperor Haile Selassie, and sponsored educational scholarships for two Ethiopian students he later adopted.[42]

Smallwood E. Williams, who broke with Lawson in 1957 to found and serve as presiding bishop of Bible Way Church of Our Lord Jesus Christ World-Wide, displayed this same sustained pattern of protest against injustice. He contended that black Pentecostal pastors should be politically active and, from his strategic Washington, DC vantage point, became a local and national political force. His advocacy included leading the city's first sit-in against segregated schools, helping found Citizens Against Police Brutality, heading the local NAACP chapter, serving as president of the D.C. chapter of the Southern Christian Leadership Conference, and as vice-chair of the Democratic Central Committee. Williams applied the same prescription of faith and self-restraint to social problems as to personal holiness. "Our whole society is looking for an ethical and moral balance in our lives," Williams contended, and further insisted that "the solution to the social ills within the black community including street crimes and drug addiction rests in people finding moral balance in their lives."[43]

Chicago activist and pastor, Arthur Brazier, crossed denominational lines to improve the quality of life in the Woodlawn neighborhood surrounding his church. Brazier

---

[42]See Arthur M Anderson, ed., *For The Defense of The Gospel: Writings of Bishop R.C. Lawson*. New York, NY: Church of Our Lord Jesus Christ, 1972; Robert C Spellman and Mabel L. Thomas, *The Life, Legend, and Legacy of Bishop R. C. Lawson*. Scotch Plains, NJ: Privately Printed, 1983; Robert C. Spellman, *Facts and Photos About Our Founders: Bishop R.C. Lawson and Mother Carrie F. Lawson*. Gainesville, FL: Displays For Schools, Inc., 1998; and Alexander C. Stewart, and Sherry Sherrod DuPree. *The Silent Spokesman: Bishop Robert Clarence Lawson*. Gainesville, FL: Displays For Schools, Inc., 1994.

[43] Smallwood Edmond Williams. *This is my Story: A Significant Life Struggle - Autobiography of Smallwood Edmond Williams*. Washington, DC: Wm. Willoughby Publishers, 1981.

became the spokesman for the Temporary Woodlawn Organization (TWO), organized by Nicholas Von Hoffman of Sol Alinsky's Industrial Areas Foundation. In 1963, Brazier successfully led TWO against the expansion of the University of Chicago into his church's Southside Chicago neighborhood. With Bill Berry of the Chicago Urban League, Brazier also formed the Coordinating Council of Community Organizations fighting segregation in Chicago's public schools. He resigned in 1965, but was active with Al Raby in facilitating Martin Luther King's 1966 visit to Chicago. Ten years later, Brazier founded the Woodlawn Preservation and Investment Corporation and the Fund for Community Redevelopment and Revitalization.[44]

Black leaders were not the only early Pentecostals interested in promoting a more just church. As the first General Overseer of the Church of God (Cleveland, TN), Ambrose Jessup (A. J.) Tomlinson drew on his Spirit-empowerment and Quaker egalitarian sensitivities to support broader opportunities for African American involvement in the denomination. As early as the 1920s, Tomlinson appointed several black ministers to leadership positions beyond the African American churches, including as overseers of states that were not entirely black and on subcommittees of the General Assembly. These appointments caused division within the leadership ranks and reportedly was, at least partially, implicated in his ouster from that body. As he left to form the Church of God of Prophecy, Tomlinson took several members of the parent body. Though the new body never grew to rival its parent. At least in its early years,

---

[44]See Arthur Brazier, *Black Self-Determination: The Story of the Woodlawn Organization*. Grand Rapids, MI: Wm. B. Eerdmans Publishers,1982 and Sammie Dortch, When God calls: A Biography of Bishop Arthur M. Brazier. Grand Rapids, MI: W.B. Eerdmans Publishers, 1996.

the organization evidenced a generally more egalitarian ethos, a more racially inclusive polity, and openness to women's ministry.

The Witness of Women

Despite the prophetic witness of these early leaders, many were woefully short in shaping a lasting, liberative word toward women within the church or society. Too often, the struggle for racial or economic justice was the myopic focus of the moment, so they did not see failure to grant full liberty to women in the church and society as a form of injustice. Indeed many espoused a biblical warrant for the second-class status they imposed on their sisters.[45]

Seymour espoused his vision of women's freedom in ministry with the same vigor as his vision for racial justice, and feely acknowledged women's role in building his mission.[46] He was adamant that this freedom had been bestowed on women since they were privy to the same Holy Spirit anointing as their brothers, using for his model the paradigm of the upper room episode when both men and women gathered and waited to receive "the oil of the Holy Ghost."[47] Seymour was determine that this stamp of God's approval on women was enough to qualify them for all levels of ministry. So, initially, extraordinary women such as Lucy Farrow, Florence Crawford, Clara Lum, and his wife, Lucy Evans Seymour, took on major ministerial and administrative responsibilities.

---

[45] for example, Robert Clarence Lawson, "A Woman Shall Compass A Man" in Alexander Stewart, ed. *Add Thou to It: Selected Works of Robert Clarence Lawson.* Lanham, MD: Seymour Press, 2019, 165-170.

[46] For a full discussion of the role of women in Seymour's ministry, see Estrelda Alexander, *The Women of Azusa Street.* Lanham, MD: Seymour Press, 2012.

[47] Untitled Article *Apostolic Faith* 1:10 (Dec 1907), 4.

Yet, despite his indebtedness to several women in assisting with the mission, in the end, he felt disheartened by the betrayal of female colleagues, fell short of the vision of gender equality, and showed growing reluctance to grant women complete parity. In formalizing the doctrinal statement of the Azusa Street Mission, Seymour distinguished men and women's roles in worship and ministry and insisted that specific liturgical duties should only be entrusted to male 'bishops.'[48] This change in position suggests that there were already restrictions on the ministry levels to which women might aspire. The language implies that ranks of elder and then bishop were limited to men; women could serve in lower positions with less ministerial privilege.

Most women settled for this lot, buying into spiritualized rhetoric that, essentially, cast them as second-class members of the body of Christ. Yet several joined their voices to the cloud of witnesses to demand their spiritual inheritance be acknowledged and respected. Just as Amanda Berry Smith and her ministry sisters, Julia Foote and Jarena Lee, would do within the Holiness movement, these women stood on their sanctified and Spirit-empowered witness as a testimony to their right to participate fully in the church's life and ministry.

Ida Bell Robinson, the founder of Mount Sinai Holy Church, expressly felt called to empower other women in response to the injustice of the United Holy Church withholding ordination from them. As a result, she created a

---

[48] In *Doctrines and Disciplines of the Azusa Street Mission of Los Angeles California*, published in 1915, Seymour insisted that "all ordination must be done by men not women. Women may be ministers but not... baptize or ordain in this work." Further, the liturgy that Seymour developed for the ordination service spells out that all laying on of hands and prayer within such service was to be done by [male] "elders." See Dale T. Irvin, "Drawing all Together in One Bond of Love: The Ecumenical Vision of William J. Seymour and the Azusa Street Revival," *Journal of Pentecostal Theology*, 6 (1995), 47.

body that, over the next seventy years, would see women serve at its helm.[49] Robinson was also an outspoken critic of racial oppression and challenged the Southern white church to renounce racist attitudes and practices.[50]

White revivalists Alma White, Florence Crawford, Aimee Semple McPherson,[51] and black women, including Mary Magdalena Tate, Eva Lambert, and Rosa Horn, followed Robinson's course in establishing denominations without gender restriction.[52] Several women, including Mozella Cook and Ernestine Cleveland Reems, made strategic decisions to branch off from the male-dominated COGIC to stand for women's equality. Cook left that body, where women were excluded from pastoral leadership, to establish and lead the Sought Out Church of God in Christ.[53] Again, refusing to be limited by the denominational structure, Reems, the daughter of a prominent COGIC bishop, first ministered as a traveling evangelist, then established a national ministry to support women, the E.C. Reems Women's International Ministries.[54]

---

[49] Elmira Jeffries served from 1946 until her death in 1964. She was succeeded by Mary Jackson, who retired in 1980 and was succeeded by Amy Stevens who served until her death in 2000, when Ruth Satchell served for one year.

[50] See for example, "Economic Justice" in the May 3, 1935, issue of her denomination's newsletter, *Latter Day Messenger* and Estrelda Alexander, "Ida Bell Robinson" in *Limited Liberty: The Legacy of Four Pentecostal Women Pioneers*. Lanham, MD: Seymour Press, 2020, 141-172.

[51] However White, founder of the Pillar of Fire was an avowed racist. Crawford founded the Apostolic Faith Mission after breaking with Seymour.

[52] Tate established the Church of the Living God Pillar and Ground of the Truth, Lambert established St. Mark's Holy Church, and Horn established the Pentecostal Faith Church for All Nations.

[53] Not much else is known about Cook or her denomination.

[54] Martha C Taylor, "Ernestine Cleveland Reems" in *From Labor to Reward: Black Church Beginnings in San Francisco, Oakland, Berkeley, And Richmond, 1849-1972*. Eugene, OR: Resource Publications, 2016..

In an era when fundamentalist white Protestants freely expressed anti-black sentiments, McPherson's Angelus Temple held interracial worship services that ignored legal restrictions. She brought black leaders to its pulpit and allowed all races to attend her meetings across the country—even in the South. Several blacks served in leadership roles in these meetings, working in the music ministry, as prayer counselors, or altar workers. Further, her Lighthouse Institute for Foursquare Evangelism (L.I.F.E.) Bible College admitted black students and encouraged black members of Angelus Temple to enroll.[55] Economic disparity also roused McPherson's attention. Throughout the Great Depression, her megachurch opened a commissary that provided food, clothing, and blankets and created soup kitchens, free clinics, and other support mechanisms to sustain an estimated 1.5 million needy people. Without distinguishing between "deserving" and "undeserving" citizens and immigrants, Christians or non-Christians, it reportedly assisted more families than other Los Angeles public or private institutions of its day.[56]

New York City's Leoncia Rosado Rousseau, called "Mama Leo" by her followers, who embraced prophetic pastoral service during the 1930s, was among the earliest Pentecostals to engage in active community service in that city. Shattering gender barriers in a then closed vocation, Rousseau was the first Latina Pentecostal pastor in New York. Her Damascus Christian Youth Crusade was the first

---

[55] There were four black students in the first class and thirty-six graduated from the college in the 20's and 30's. Most found places to minister at Angelus Temple, while others started congregations outside the Foursquare movement. For unlike with McPherson's openness, the earliest black graduates of the college did not receive Foursquare pastoral appointments.

[56] See Estrelda Alexander, "Amy Semple McPherson" in *Limited Liberty: The Legacy of Four Pentecostal Women Pioneers.* Lanham, MD: Seymour Press, 2020, 107-139.

Protestant church-sponsored program to campaign against drug abuse there. Because of its effectiveness, this program garnered wide recognition and became a state-wide model.[57]

Rousseau was not the first Latina woman to marry Spirit-empowered evangelism with community engagement. Before arriving at Azusa Street, Susie Villa Valdez, a devout Catholic who converted to Pentecostalism under Yoakum's ministry, worked with him at Pisgah House. After her Azusa Street encounter, she broadened her ministry by moving out to the Los Angeles slums and migrant labor camps of Redlands, Riverside, and San Bernardino to witness to hundreds of Latinos swarming into these areas as cheap labor. Her witness among the Spanish community was instrumental in drawing many to the Azusa Street meetings and Pentecostal faith.[58]

During the Depression, the largely uneducated and self-taught, Lucinda Madden (Lucy) Smith formed alliances with prominent Chicago businessmen to carry out a substantial outreach ministry throughout the city's South Side, becoming the city's first African American pastor to regularly distribute food and clothing without regard to race. Smith also formed alliances with other black churches in Chicago's Bronzeville section, even while many male pastors opposed women's ministry and leadership.[59]

During the same time, Rosa Artimus Horn established the Gleaners' Aid Home to regularly feed thousands of Harlem's poor. From the 1940s through the 1970s, Horn provided

---

[57] Virginia Sanchez Korrol, "In Search of Unconventional Women," in Vicki L. Ruiz, ed., *Unequal Sisters: An Inclusive Reader in U.S. Women's History*. New York: Routledge, 2000.

[58] A. C. Valdez, *Fire on Azusa Street: An Eyewitness Account*. Costa Mesa, CA: Gift Publications, 1980.

[59] Wallace Best, "A Woman's Work an Urban World" in *Passionately Human No Less Divine: Religion and Culture in Black Chicago, 1915-1952*. Princeton, NJ: Princeton University Press, 2007, 147-180.

vocational and religious training to poor youth while she vociferously defended women's leadership in the church.[60]

At its height, Charleszetta Waddles' Perpetual Mission for Saving Souls of All Nations in Detroit sheltered the homeless, annually served between 90,000 and 100,000 meals for thirty-five cents, and provided emergency financial assistance, job training, an arts program, and a culinary education program all without government funding.[61]

Contemporary Witnesses

As the renewal movement has matured, it has begun to produce a cadre of leaders who deliberately mesh their distinct spirituality with a progressive social consciousness. Though not representing the majority, they tackle complex issues at the expense of being marked as "liberal" or even "radical" by more conservative elements. Still, while casting themselves as theologically conservative, many remain in the movement to give voice to future generations.

Some, however, like James A Forbes, Jr., a child of classical Pentecostalism,[62] have distanced themselves without denouncing renewal spirituality. Forbes previously pastored two United Holy Church of America congregations, but in 1989, became the first African American, and only Pentecostal, senior minister of New York's prestigious Riverside Church, one of the country's largest multicultural, interdenominational congregations. While no longer singly aligned with classical Pentecostalism, Forbes never forsook

---

[60] Bettye Collier-Thomas, "Rosa Artimus Horn" in *Daughters of Thunder: Black Women Preachers and their Sermons, 1850-1979*. San Francisco, CA: Jossey-Bass, 1998, 173-176.

[61] Darlene Clark, Hine, "Charleszetta Waddles" in *Black Women in America: An Historical Encyclopedia. Brooklyn*. New York: Carlson Publishing, Inc., 1993.

[62] Forbes was raised and was ordained in the United Holy Church of America where his father had served as presiding bishop.

roots shaped within that spirituality. He identified himself as a "progressive Pentecostal" who holds a "strong emphasis on spirit, but a deep commitment to transformative social action" two decades before Miller and Yamamori used the phrase.[63] Forbes led Riverside's work with a consortium of churches in Harlem's redevelopment and supported the Harlem Week of Prayer for Healing of AIDS. In his 2010 work, *Whose Gospel: A Concise Guide to Progressive Protestantism*, he addressed the crucial issues of our time—poverty, war, women's equality, racial justice, sexuality, and the environment and offered a vision of progressive social change.[64]

Herbert Daughtry, former Presiding Minister of The House of the Lord Churches, is known for his school integration activism and work with Operation Breadbasket, the Coalition of Concerned Leaders, and Citizens to Save Our Jobs, and, in 1977, led a boycott of Brooklyn businesses to obtain jobs and services for African Americans.[65] While remaining Pentecostal, he founded the African People's Christian Organization to create an African Christian nation by highlighting both African origins and biblical teachings. His involvement has included assisting Civil Rights Movement leader, Jesse Jackson's presidential bid and accompanying him to the Vatican to advocate for human rights. He also participated in mayor, David Dinkins' delegation to South Africa to meet with Nelson and Winnie

---

[63] See James A Forbes, Jr. *The Holy Spirit and Preaching*. Nashville, TN: Abingdon Press, 1989; also his "Shall we Call the Dream Progressive Pentecostalism" *Spirit: A Journal of Issues Incidental to Black Pentecostalism*, 1:1 (1977), 31-35; and Donald Miller and Tetsunao Yamamori, *Global Pentecostalism: The New Face of Christian Social Engagement*. Oakland, CA: University of California Press, 2007.

[64] James A. Forbes, *Whose Gospel: A Concise Guide to Progressive Protestantism*. New York: New Press 2010.

[65] His *No Monopoly on Suffering: Blacks and Jews in Crown Heights and Elsewhere* dealt with the 1991 crisis in ethnic tensions in that neighborhood.

Mandella and led a multi-faith delegation on a peace-seeking mission to Iraq. His founding and leading several justice organizations and has made him an international spokesperson on global injustice.

Michael McBride, pastor of West Berkeley, California's multiracial The Way Christian Center, directs the LIVE FREE Campaign of inter-faith organizations and congregations addressing violence and crime. Further, he co-founded the Community Justice Reform Coalition and the National Black Brown Gun Violence Prevention Consortium, two organizations that also address mass incarceration of young people of color. McBride regularly contributes to media, serves on local and national task forces, and is active with ecumenical efforts on faith, racial justice, and community engagement. In addition, he tackles issues such as LGBQT justice that many renewalists refuse to address, and is involved at the street level, even being arrested for causes.[66]

South African bishop Frank Chikane's prophetic anti-apartheid activism has come at great personal cost, even within his denomination, the Apostolic Faith Mission. At one time, his advocacy for the denomination's African constituency led to his suspension. Moreover, South African authorities have repeatedly detained Chikane, and at one point, he was tried for treason, though charges were later dropped. The year that he was elected General Secretary of the South African Council of Churches (SACC), the police

---

[66] See Richard L. Wood and Brad R. Fulton, "Challenge to America: An Interview with Rev. Michael McBride, Lifelines to Healing LiveFree Campaign, PICO" in *A Shared Future: Faith-Based Organizing for Racial Equity and Ethical Democracy*. Chicago, IL: University of Chicago Press, 2015, and Dani Gabriel, "Where Faith-Based and Secular Organizers Find Common Ground" *Sojourners*, October 4, 2028. https://sojo.net/articles/where-faith-based-and-secular-organizers-find-common-ground.

began harassing the organization, going as far as raiding their offices.⁶⁷

Pastor and gynecologist, Denis Mukwege, received the 2018 Nobel Peace Prize for his work to end sexual violence as a weapon of war in the Democratic Republic of Congo. For twenty preceding years, his Panzi Hospital treated over 50,000 survivors of such violence. His medical team developed a model for treating wartime rape by integrating psychological, legal, and socio-economic support for victims.⁶⁸

Ethiopian Pentecostal, Prime Minister Abiy Ali, was honored with the same prize for leading that country in resuming peace talks with neighboring Eritrea after a 20-year post-war stalemate. He also worked to reconcile the two branches of the Ethiopian Orthodox Church, which split in 1991, and to reconcile Muslims and Christians in his hometown of Beshasha. In addition, his reforms include granting amnesty to political prisoners, discontinuing media censorship, legalizing opposition groups, dismissing corrupt military and civilian leaders, increasing women's social and political influence, and pledging free and fair elections. He also worked to normalize diplomatic relations between Eritrea and Djibouti and mediated the protracted conflict between Kenya and Somalia over a disputed marine area.⁶⁹

---

⁶⁷ See Frank Chikane, *No Life of My Own*. Johannesburg, SA: Picador Africa, 2012.

⁶⁸ Kate Shellnutt, "Nobel Peace Prize Goes to Christian Doctor Who Heals Rape Victims" *Christianity Today. October 5, 2018. https://www.christianitytoday.com/news/2018/october/denis-mukwege-congo-nobel-peace-prize.html.*

⁶⁹ See Campbell Campbell-Jack, "Abiy Ahmed Ali, Ethiopian Prime Minister, Nobel Peace Prize Winner and an Evangelical" *Christianity Today* December 11, 2019. https://www.christiantoday.com/article/abiy-ahmed-ali-ethiopian-prime-minister-nobel-peace-prize-winner-and-an-evangelical/133802.htm or "Ethiopia's Prime Minister Pastor Abiy Ahmed Wins 2019

Ecumenist, Joe Aldred, retired as a bishop in the Church of God of Prophecy in Great Britain but is still actively concerned with community development, interfaith relations, education, and health. As Secretary for Minority Ethnic Christian Affairs (MECA) at Churches Together in England and Director of Britain's Centre for Black and White Christian Partnership.[70] Aldred defined himself as interested in "issues that lead to flourishing for all, particularly within the African and Diaspora communities in the United Kingdom and the Caribbean."[71]

Another British ecumenist, Jamaican-born Joel Edwards, made history as the first black General Director of the Evangelical Alliance. The organization of over one million Christians unites churches on common goals and lobbies the British government. As a key leader within the Jamaican Diaspora, Edwards received the 2003 Jamaican Prime Minister's Medal of Appreciation. Two years later, he received an Honorary Doctorate in Divinity from the Caribbean Graduate School of Theology. Until his death in 2021, Edwards was a regular broadcaster with international media outlets, and a member of Britain's Advisory Board on Human Rights and Religious Freedom.[72]

Nobel Peace Prize" *Believer's Portal* October 17, 2019. https://believersportal.com/ethiopias-prime-minister-pastor-abiy-ahmed-wins-nobel-peace-prize/

[70] His previous works include *The Black Church in the 21st Century*. London: Darton, Longman & Todd, 2010 and *Respect: Understanding Caribbean British Christianity*. London: Epworth, 2005.

[71] "About Joe" https://drjoealdred.info/.

[72] Morgan Lee, "Died: Joel Edwards, the First Black Evangelical Alliance UK Head" Christianity Today, July 6, 2021. https://www.christianitytoday.com/news/2021/july/died-joel-edwards-evangelical-association-united-kingdom.html.

Spurring Us On

For early Pentecostal leaders, as for us, justice-seeking was not God's option for those bent toward the prophetic, nor a selection from a menu of Christian virtues. But, like the call to evangelism, worship, and prayer, the call to justice-seeking is essential for those who gather to study, deliberate, and invoke the name of Christ. It is an undeniable, inescapable unction imparted with the gift of the Holy Spirit. Yet, such visible engagement did not always survive the movement's initial stages for several reasons.

First, Pentecostalism unfolded simultaneously with Darwinism, higher criticism, the social gospel, and ecumenism movements. Threatened by the perceived potential of these movements to destabilize biblical Christianity, Pentecostals joined other evangelicals to protest against these "modernist" tendencies and "false doctrines." The fear was that the social gospel would substitute social work for grace and social transformation for personal salvation.

Secondly, early adherents suffered heavy persecution, including taunting, bearing such derogatory monikers as "holy rollers," and being shunned by "respectable" religious folks who often considered them demon-possessed or insane. Physical beatings and arson against members were not uncommon. In turn, Pentecostals often shunned the outside world, seeing most non-believers as hostile, hopelessly lost, and worldly.

Finally, the Holiness-Pentecostal movement and subsequent renewal iterations shifted the earlier pre-millennial optimism to a post-millennial pessimism regarding bringing structural change in the surrounding society. Thus, the character of the movement changed vis-à-vis that society. The most one could hope for was rescuing those few who would look for Christ's return and establishment of the new Kingdom.

Early renewalists represented the lower classes. The un- and undereducated African Americans, Hispanics, and other minorities had a higher representation than the middle- and upper classes, the highly educated or whites. With age has come a degree of dialogue with other Christian traditions and some movement toward ecumenism. Though still considered an oddity in some circles, modern Pentecostalism draws its rank from a broader segment of society than the "disinherited"[73] members among whom it was first popular and has gained a semblance of respectability and acceptance. Second and third-generation Pentecostals have moved increasingly into the social and economic mainstream, and Pentecostal spirituality is infiltrating mainline congregations via the Charismatic and Neo-Pentecostal movements. So, according to historian, Vinson Synan,

> By the 1930s, it became clear that the great appeal of the... movement would be to the lower classes [but]... once these classes rose up the economic scale, the socio-cultural character of the movement would rise with it.[74]

Unfortunately, in that rise, many renewalists forgot or sought to separate themselves from the sting of oppression, and in doing so, some failed to keep in mind the mandate of the Spirit to seek justice.

---

[73] A characterization used by Robert Mapes Anderson in *Vision of the Disinherited: The Making of American Pentecostalism.* Peabody, MA: Hendrickson Publications, 1992.

[74] Vinson Synan, *The Holiness-Pentecostal Movement*, Plainfield, NJ: Logos International, 1975, 200.

The Witness of Renewal Scholarship

Assuredly, the impetus for justice-seeking comes first from Scripture. Yet, a growing cadre of those with love for the Church and the renewal movement has produced a body of scholarly work regarding issues involved in justice-seeking that spurs conversation and offers biblical and theological possibilities for solutions. This important work is not scholarship for its own sake, but is an effort by the sons and daughters of the movement to aid our communities in wrestling with the issues that they previously avoided. Though not always appreciated, renewal scholars write with both the Church and academy in mind, and their works serves as resources for pastors, church leaders, and others who desire to understand the struggle for justice.

Fifty years ago, the seemingly oxymoronic terms' Pentecostal' or 'renewal' and 'scholarship' were rarely heard together. Further, detractors have noted the movement's historical rejection of theological training and general criticism of academia. Hence, many outsiders see the renewal movement as contributing nothing to the theological endeavor or developing no solid responses to justice issues. Moreover, emerging Pentecostal scholarship initially focused on doctrine, apologetics, practical theology, biblical studies, ecclesiology, and eschatology. Within a short time, church history and missiology began to be explored. However, efforts to develop a systematic theology or substantially address religion and culture or ethics are relatively recent and remain suspect to some denominational leadership.

Yet, contemporary renewal scholars exists throughout the breadth of the movement — Holiness, classical Pentecostal, Charismatic, and Neo-Pentecostal are working within a variety of academic specialties—anthropology, biblical studies, ethics, religion and culture, ecumenism, and theology, and ancillary disciplines. They are applying their Spirit-empowered scholarship and God-given intellectual prowess to investigate issues of justice in classrooms, conference podiums, and publishing efforts.

Many feel called to both the church and the academy. Yet, in their willingness to stand against their educational institutions and denominations to honestly confront national and global justice concerns in their classrooms, from conference podiums and in their publishing efforts, these scholars have use their God-given intellectual prowess to develop a body of work that shows a nuanced and authentic approach to these vital concerns.

Their efforts coalesced in the formation of organizations that have explicit commtments to justice seeking interest. The Society for Pentecostal Studies was formed over fifty years ago. Since then, it has become a global, interdenominational, multi-ethnic, gender-inclusive, and multi-generational organization. Scholars from religiously affiliated colleges, graduate students from secular institutions, and a variety of independent researchers gather at its Annual Meeting and use its peer-reviewed journal, *Pneuma*, to wrestle with issues. Its efforts have been joined by several scholarly/Pentecostal bodies around the globe,[75] as well as by organizations such as the Alliance of Black Pentecostal Scholars, Pentecostals for Peace and Justice, and the Pentecostal Justice Coalition.[76]

---

[75] These include European Pentecostal Theological Association, the Asia Pacific Theological Seminary in the Philippines, and Association for Pentecostal Theological Education in Africa. Their offerings of their journals have been augmented by those of H*ECHOS*, offering Spanish language articles on Pentecostalism, the *Journal for Pentecostal Theology, PentecoStudies: Online Journal for the Interdisciplinary Study of Pentecostal and Charismatic Movements, Pneuma Review*, and *Spiritus: ORU Journal of Theology*:

[76] Many members of SPS are also aligned with these groups.

Some Renewal Scholars

Among the earliest Pentecostals of any race to receive an earned doctorate, Bennie E. Goodwin worked primarily in the Church of God in Christ, centered on the intersection between education and justice, and saw education as a vehicle for social change. Though his more than twenty books spanned a breadth of academic and ecclesial subjects, he focused on lifting up black achievement and spurring fellow clergy to become theologically trained. He served as a vice president of the National Association of Black Evangelicals, participated in the National Association for the Advancement of Colored People (NAACP), and worked with the Southern Christian Leadership Conference when many Pentecostals viewed these as liberal organizations that should be avoided.[77]

Controversial political scientist, James S. Tinney, challenged the renewal community's response to race relations and, what he saw as, its unjust response to the homosexual community. Shortly before his untimely death, in 1979, Tinney launched *Spirit: A Journal of Issues Incident to Black Pentecostalism*. Though published for only two years, within its pages, leading voices and budding black scholars spoke prophetically to issues of their time. However, after Tinney openly promoted his more liberal stance on homosexuality, his voice was essentially silenced within the movement. Yet he continued defining himself as Pentecostal, while he founded the Pentecostal Coalition for Human Rights[78] and an open and affirming congregation. However,

---

[77] See, for example, Bennie E. Goodwin, "Social Implications of Pentecostal Power" *Spirit: A Journal of Issues Incident to Black Pentecostalism* 1:1, 31-35, and his *Reflections on Education: Meditations on King, Friere and Jesus as Social and Religious Educators*. East Orange, NJ: Goodpatrick Publishers, 1978.

[78] An organization that Tinney established support homosexual and lesbian efforts for greater inclusion within the Pentecostal movement. For information

his work also addressed structural inequality and academic racism. Moreover, he pioneered the study of the African American origins of Pentecostalism and has been instrumental in restoring William Seymour to his place of prominence within the movement.[79]

In 1970, ethicist, Leonard Lovett served as founding Dean of the Charles H. Mason Theological Seminary at the Interdenominational Theological Center (ITC), an institution of the Atlanta University Center consortium. His outspoken forays into the fields of justice and ecumenism distinguished him as willing to forego the traditional arenas of limitedly acceptable exploration to delve into issues many other Pentecostals skirted. His attacks on historical racism both within the movement as well as within the broader society often placed him at odds with both his black Pentecostal community and white scholars.[80]

In 1997, nearly a quarter century after Lovett left the institution, sociologist, Robert Franklin, became its sixth president before serving as the tenth president of Morehouse College, the nation's largest private, four-year men's liberal arts college. In addition, he was a program officer in the Ford Foundation's Human Rights and Social Justice Program,

---

on Tinney see Kittredge Cherry, "James Tinney: Black Gay Professor who Founded LGBTQ Church in 1982" *QSpirit* Jun 17, 2021. https://qspirit.net/james-tinney-black-lgbtq-church/.

[79] See James S. Tinney, "Black Origins of the Pentecostal Movement" *Christianity Today* 16 (October 8, 1971), 6 and "William J. Seymour: Father of Modern-Day Pentecostalism," in Randall Burkett and Richard Newman, eds., *Black Apostles: Afro-American Clergy Confront the Twentieth Century.* Boston: G.K. Hall, 1978, 213-225.

[80] See, for example, Leonard Lovett, "Perspective on the Black Origins of the Contemporary Pentecostal Movement," *Journal of the Interdenominational Theological Center* 1:1 (1973), 36-49 and "The Present: The Problem of Racism in the Contemporary Pentecostal Movement" *Cyberjournal For Pentecostal-Charismatic Research.* 14 (May 2005). http://www.pctii.org/cyberj/cyberj14/lovett1.html.

where he was responsible for grants to African American churches that were engaged in social service delivery and for advising the president of the Foundation about such issues.

Since the 1990s, prolific, white New Testament scholar, Craig Keener, an ordained minister in an African-American Baptist church has been an outspoken justice advocate. While continuing prolific scholarship on women's equality[81] and racial reconciliation in the United States and Africa,[82] Keener employs thorough scriptural exegesis to defend his position on justice in his more than twenty-five books and more than 200 essays and articles he has produced to date.

Anthropologist, Craig Scandrett-Leatherman founded Faith for Justice in St. Louis, an organization that encourages biblical activism through cooperative efforts between the church and the community. Though ordained in the Free Methodist Church, his scholarship has often focused on racial justice within the renewal context, and he has authored numerous articles on the subject. In addition, his concern for ecological justice led him to co-found The Urban EcoBlock, an activist group that reclaims urban areas to create socially responsible, environmentally healthy spaces.[83]

Ecumenist, Cheryl Bridges-Johns has worked to span the gap between historic Protestant Christianity and emerging forms of renewal Christianity. These efforts have involved her

---

[81] Craig S. Keener, "Women in Ministry: Another Egalitarian Perspective" in James R. Beck, ed., *Two Views on Women in Ministry*, Nashville, TN: Zondervan Academic, 2005; and *Paul, Women, and Wives: Marriage and Women's Ministry in the Letters of Paul*. Waco, TX: Baker Academic, 1992.

[82] Craig S. Keener, "Some New Testament Invitations to Ethnic Reconciliation." *Evangelical Quarterly*. 75:3, (2003), 195–213. See also, Craig Keener and Médine Moussounga Keener. *Impossible Love: The True Story of an African Civil War, Miracles and Hope against All Odds*. Royal Oak, MI: Chosen Books, 2016.

[83] For information on the organization visit the Urban EcoBlock website at https://urbanecoblock.org/about/who-we-are/

in such projects as the International Roman Catholic-Pentecostal Dialogue, Evangelicals and Catholics Together (ECT), and the Commission on Faith and Order for the National Council of Churches. In addition, her concern for environmental issues involves working with the Center for Health and the Global Environment at Harvard Medical School and the National Association of Evangelicals. For more than three decades, Bridges-Johns has also actively advocated for women within the Pentecostal movement and served as a mentor and role model for countless younger women in the academy, the renewal movement, and broader faith communities.[84]

Pastor and ethicist, Murray Dempster, has focused on social concerns throughout his career within the Pentecostal Academy.[85] He posits that speaking in tongues—the central connecting ritual of classical Pentecostals, Charismatics, and Neo-Pentecostals—is a God-ordained vehicle for breaking down barriers between Christians.[86] Dempster, who has written numerous scholarly articles and book chapters and co-edited and co-authored three books, also Served as editor of *Pneuma: the Journal of the Society for Pentecostal Studies*.

Samuel Solivan began work as a community organizer in East Harlem and has continued to actively pursue both practical and scholarly solutions to problems that plague our society. While still a graduate student in Holland, Michigan,

---

[84] See Cheryl Bridges-Johns, *Pentecostal Formation: A Pedagogy among the Oppressed*. Eugene, OR: Wipf and Stock, 2010.

[85] Murray W. Dempster, "Christian Social Concern In Pentecostal Perspective: Reformulating Pentecostal Eschatology." *Journal of Pentecostal Theology* 2(1993), 51-64, and "Evangelism, Social Concern and the Kingdom of God" in Murray W. Dempster, Byron D. Klaus, and Douglas Petersen, eds., *Called and Empowered: Global Mission in Pentecostal Perspective*. Waco, TX: Baker Books, 1991.

[86] Murray W. Dempster, "The Church's Moral Witness: A Study of Glossolalia in Luke's Theology of Acts" *Paraclete* 23 (1989), 1-7.

Solivan was named Commissioner of Education and Housing for its Human Relations Commission and started the West Michigan Latino Ministers Association. He went on to complete his doctorate before penning his major work, *Spirit, Pathos, and Liberation: Toward an Hispanic Pentecostal Theology*, in which he advocated for justice in the mainland United States and Puerto Rico.[87] Further, he has participated in various ecumenical efforts, including dialogues between Pentecostals and the World Council of Churches. His involvement in academia has included serving on the faculties at New York Theological Seminary and Boston University, as well as Vice President of the Inter-American University of Puerto Rico.

The *National Catholic Reporter* named social ethicist, Eldin Villafañe,[88] founding director of the Center for Urban Ministerial Education, among the nation's ten most influential Hispanic religious leaders. In *The Liberating Spirit: Toward an Hispanic American Pentecostal Social Ethic*, he argued that Latino/a Pentecostalism, in all its complexity, needed to be understood as a Spirit-led, prophetic justice movement, particularly in urban settings. Villafañe engages biblical texts in promoting ethical theologizing and action. He also critiques the "prosperity gospel" while advocating a consistent pneumatology that engenders a spirituality that does not separate evangelism from justice.[89]

---

[87] See Samuel Solivan. *Spirit, Pathos and Liberation: Toward an Hispanic Pentecostal Theology* (*Journal of Pentecostal Theology Su*pplement). New York: Bloomsbury T&T Clark, 1998.

[88] See Eldin Villafañe, *Seek the Peace of the City: Reflections on Urban Ministry* Grand Rapids, MI: William B. Eerdmans Publishers, 1995 and *The Liberating Spirit: Toward an Hispanic American Pentecostal Social Ethic*. Rapids, MI: Wm. B. Eerdmans, 1993.

[89] Efraín Agosto, "Scripture and Liberating Ethics: Honoring Eldin Villafañe" *Lexington Theological Quarterly*, (2018), 59-67
https://www.lextheo.edu/wp-content/uploads/2018/10/File-6-Agosto-1.pdf

Outspoken public intellectual and Afro-British theologian, Robert Beckford, teaches in schools, prisons, and community centers; advises government departments and international bodies; and is Britain's first tutor in black theology. Though raised within Britain's New Testament Church of God, Beckford has produced several documentaries that offer his ecumenical audience a stinging critique of historical interpretations of Christian faith, racially-biased theologies, and the Church's lack of engagement with contemporary culture.[90]

There is a growing cadre of justice engaged renewal scholars—Kim Alexander, Kenneth Archer, Daniela Augustine, Lisa Bowen, Jonathan Chism, Clifton Clarke, Dale Coulter, Gastón Espinosa, Chris Greene, Antipas Harris, Nestor Medina, Steven Studebaker, Miroslav Volf, Wolfgang Vondey, Michael Wilkinson, Nimi Wariboko, Elton Weaver, and Amos Young stand among (not over against) others.[91]

---

[90] See, for example, *Jesus is Dread: Black Theology and Black Culture in Britain*. London: Darton, Longman, and Todd. 1998, and *Dread and Pentecostal: A Political Theology for the Black Church in Britain*. London: SPCK. 2000.

[91] See, for example, Kim Alexander and Hollis Gause, *Women In Leadership: A Pentecostal Perspective*. Cleveland, TN: Center for Leadership and Care, 2006; Miroslav Volf, *Exclusion and Embrace: A Theological Exploration of Identity, Otherness, and Reconciliation*. Nashville: Abingdon Press, 1996 and his "Materiality of Salvation: An Investigation in the Soteriologies of Liberation and Pentecostal Theologies," *Journal of Ecumenical Studies* 26, no. 3 (Summer 1989), 447–67; Michael Wilkinson and Steven M. Studebaker, *A Liberating Spirit*. Eugene, OR: Wipf and Stock, 2010; Nimbi Wariboko, *The Charismatic City and the Public Resurgence of Religion: A Pentecostal Social Ethics of Cosmopolitan Urban Life*. Basingstoke: Palgrave Macmillan, 2014; Elden Villafañe *The Liberating Spirit: Toward an Hispanic American Pentecostal Social Ethic*. Grand Rapids, MI: Wm. B. Eerdmans Publishing Company, 1993; Jonathan Chism, *Saints in the Struggle: Church of God in Christ Activists in the Memphis Civil Rights Movement, 1954–1968*. Lanham Lexington Books, 2021 or *The Rise to Respectability: Race, Religion, and the Church of God in Christ*. Lanham, MD: Lexington Books, 2019; and Antipas Harris and Michael Palmer, *The Spirit and Social Justice:*

Assuredly, their work does not advocate a singular stance on any issues. Yet, at the root of prophetic scholarly leadership, each exhibits a Spirit-driven, biblically informed intentionality that raises questions and drives answers for renewalists who seek justice. The work of these scholars, and the testimonies of the other Spirit-empowered witnesses present an entry point that permits broader conversation about the ongoing involvement of, at least a segment of, renewalist in the arduous task of justice seeking. Their combined witness helps contemporary renewalists navigate the current maze of justice issues in a way that continues to embrace a committed to biblical truth and the experience of Spirit-empowerment without ignoring the necessity to get involved in what to many has been untested territory.

Interdisciplinary Global Perspectives: Scripture and Theology and Vol I - *Scripture and Theology* and Vol II - *History, Race & Culture.* Lanham, MD: Seymour Press, 2019.

7

Prophetic Witness

There are people who think
There are people who do
There are people who think and do
There are those people who both think deeply and do courageously
                                                                St. Jerome

    The Gospel is not simply a message about eternal salvation for believers who persevere through some degree of suffering in this present world. Neither does it merely communicate a promise of temporal justice in the here and now. It is never an either/or proposition but is always both/and. For the same God, who is concerned about our eternal welfare, is touched by our individual infirmities and is holistically concerned for the whole world that is so loved. Just as each person is heir to a sinful nature, each is the subject of divine love. And any presentation of the Gospel that does not account for this truth is inauthentic and does not convey the full story of the good news of Jesus.
    Yet, only God's revelation of truth is completely unfettered by a fallen, distorted worldview. We all see in part and, in our fallenness, dare to express that part as a whole. It is not surprising that human renditions of the Gospel are flawed. No matter how much we protest to the contrary, our apologetic and presentations are filtered through agendas colored by how we see the world and who our audience might be.
    For example, four men with different temperaments who addressed different cultural concerns composed the four Gospel narratives. In communicating the gracious gift of

salvation in Christ, each related the story with his respective community in mind. Though each sought to convey the message of the in-breaking of God's Kingdom through the incarnate Jesus, they were careful to frame their messages in language that would appeal to their particular audience. So, none could fully comprehend or pass on the full extent of what was accomplished in Christ, yet together, they present a complete story.

As one who shared a thoroughly Hebrew consciousness, Matthew sought to convince an audience familiar with Jewish scriptures, genealogies, and controversies that Jesus was the expected Messiah. Mark wrote to Gentiles within the Roman Empire to help them understand that Jesus was indeed the Son of God. Luke, the only Greek, penned his narrative to persuade his intellectually minded readers of a Christian faith based on historically reliable and verifiable events. John's Gospel contains theological content regarding the person of Christ as both God and man to convey the meaning of faith to a broad audience. Each writer brought their limited understanding of what was unfolding, for none could relay the whole story. And, while each Gospel could convincingly stand alone for their intended constituencies, together they provide a holistic portrait and give us a fuller picture of Jesus' life and ministry.

In much the same way, every theology is crafted for a particular hearing. Further, all theology is political in some way and projects the worldview of the community to which it is addressed. Each attempt to communicate revelation is filtered through a limited understanding, colored by the community's self-interest, shared values, and expectations about who God is. Further, they share a sense of how God operates and how the world and its inhabitants should conduct themselves in relation to God and each other.

Theology, consciously or subconsciously, drives actions. How we think about God predicts how we respond to the issues of life and to each other. If we think of God as ultimately loving and just, we act justly towards our fellow humans. If we believe God is hierarchical, we attempt to maintain race, gender, and class hierarchies. If we see God as coercive, we understand that people can only be ruled by coercion.

Moreover, life experiences teach us how to think about God. If our lives have been colored by severe abuse, injustice, or oppression, especially at the hands of God's representatives, we see God having these same characteristics despite converse religious pronouncements. It is hard to think of a generous and gracious God when our entire lives have been lived in want. It is difficult to hear the Church speak of a God who is a deliverer when that same Church is implicated in our oppression. If, instead, our lives have regularly been characterized by loving, free, caring relationships, we think of a God who exhibits these characteristics.

Further, we can gauge a community's beliefs about God and eternal matters by how they conduct their lives and treat others. For, their actions ultimately confirm their belief system. Communities that treat others rigidly do so because they believe in a rigid, uncaring God. Communities that treat others with gracious kindness do so because they imagine that a merciful God is gracious and kind.

Contemporary Expressions of the Gospel

In the present moment, the message of the good news of God's in-breaking is conveyed within a world besieged by theological systems governed by predominantly secular concerns. Furthermore, a community's communication of the Gospel is dependent on its members' social and political position as much as it is concerned with eternal matters.

The Prosperity Gospel

The prosperity gospel presents a message of God's generosity toward those who are favored and adept at employing their faith to induce God to act on their behalf. This interpretation of the biblical message frames the fruit of salvation as an individualistic blessing. It conveys evidence of God's favor as individual gain, equating strong Christian faith with material success and personal goal achievement. Also designated the "word of faith" or "the health-and-wealth gospel," it presents a syncretistic blend of contemporary Pentecostal/Charismatic theology with 19th-century metaphysical New Thought. This philosophy held that Christians wield authority over their circumstances through "positive confession" which allows escape from ordinary human circumstances that bring about ill-health, poverty, or lack of success in various areas of life.

This iteration of the Gospel emphasizes idolatrous greed dressed as God's blessing, taking biblical themes of God's graciousness and divine provision to non-biblical extremes. It explains hardship as the sufferer's fault and poverty as resulting from some spiritual defect within the impoverished. Yet, while personal sin may result in poverty, this rendition of the Gospel ignores the effects of the sin of others and structural evils that may be its root cause.

Church leaders are implicated in oppression when they compel less well-off members to give beyond their means while leaders live in luxury, while the people in the pews are forced to pay late fees on credit cards, are unable to adequately feed their families, live in substandard housing and have their utilities disconnected. Moreover, this Gospel offers the most benefit to its purveyors who urge "seed-faith" giving by even the most impoverished members of their communities so that the purveyors can enrich themselves.

Those without material or financial success are deemed to merit only limited aid since God has chosen not to bless them as much as others. With this understanding, therefore, more fortunate Christians need do nothing to assist the poor. Holders of this Gospel are reluctant to seriously discuss either personal or corporate sin except as the failure to extend one's faith to grasp the principles of more abundant life. There is no call for repentance, except for lack of faith. Such teaching does not adequately consider the seriousness of the part such sin plays in bringing about our suffering as well as the suffering of others—our families, community, and world.

Importantly, no explanation is offered for personal or communal suffering inflicted by other individuals or institutional structures. Instead, this presentation upholds the status quo, insisting that lack of faith means those who suffer have not earned a better fate, and the poor have not earned a blessing sufficient to raise them out of poverty.[1] Since unnecessary suffering comes about because individuals have not operated through positive confession,[2] such theologizing fails to explain why faithful Christians sometimes suffer oppression while the unrighteous prosper.

Evangelicalism

Rigid Evangelical presentations of the Gospel pose a set of truths about the authority of Scripture, the divine and human identity of Christ, and what has been accomplished

---

[1] Anne Turner and Michael O'Hanlon, "The Prosperity Gospel's Shallow Preaching: The prosperity Gospel is Full of Promises, but Lacking in Consolations" *The National Interest*, February 5, 2017. https://nationalinterest.org/ feature/the-prosperity-gospels-shallow-preaching-19324.

[2] See Kate Bowler, *Blessed: A History of the American Prosperity Gospel.* New York: Oxford University Press, 2018.

for humankind in His atoning work on the Cross. It requires assent to a set of propositional truths and insistence on an individual's personal experience of the new birth. Often embedded in this theology is a Reform understanding that we are not only predestined to our eternal fate, but also to our predetermined temporal position. The community in which this theology is shaped values order and postulates a God-ordained social structure that maintains the existing state of affairs and is easily enlisted in the service of keeping the powerful in power.[3] With this understanding, salvation is a matter of private experience for those preordained to receive this experience that colors every aspect of life.

While affirming commitment to the trustworthiness and full authority of Scripture that produces a socially, as well as theologically, conservative worldview, often shallow reading of the text avoids attention to the "weightier matters of the Law" and often overlooks concern for authentic justice. This engagement of Scripture often reverts to biblical literalism, or biblicism, that insists that this is the only correct reading. As such, it leaves no room for alternative readings that lead to different interpretations of contemporary issues.

The tendency toward radical individualism restricts belief to a matter of private experience, increasingly filtered through a distinctive worldview, and withdrawn from engaging public issues of no personal consequence for the believer's everyday life. This faith does not ask tough questions regarding how we situate ourselves in the world vis-à-vis those who are less fortunate or different from us in some significant way. Rather, it evidences an inbred

---

[3] Elizabeth Fox-Genovese and Eugene D. Genovese, "The Divine Sanction of Social Order: Religious Foundations of the Southern Slaveholders' World View." *Journal of the American Academy of Religion* 55:2 (Summer, 1987), 211-233.

schizophrenic dualism that views the Church and the world as two separate, unrelated spheres. Simultaneously, within the American context, it weds faith to the "democratic" experiment and characterizes the country as a "Christian nation" actuated by "Judeo-Christian values." As Evangelical leaders became less interested in traditional doctrine and more interested in moralistic therapeutic deism, they shaped a Church of what Pew Research calls "God-and-Country Believers" who may not, often, attend Church or be interested in, or aware of, traditional Christian beliefs. But they believe in God and America.[4]

Forerunners of Evangelicalism did not neglect issues of justice. Calvin insisted it was not enough to live a pious life, but God's Law "is kept only when men are just, and kind, and true, towards each other… give[ing] proper and sufficient evidence of sincere piety."[5] John Wesley and his followers stood vehemently against the institution of slavery and called for its abolition, for charity toward the poor, and for women's rights and suffrage, seeing these as distinctly biblical issues. Taking their cue from Wesley, radical Holiness leaders upheld Evangelical tenets, and included attention to justice.

Early Pentecostal theology borrowed its ethical framework from this tradition. Yet, again, contemporary iterations of Evangelicalism lack the ethical rigor to bring the Scripture to bear on issues not deemed of personal consequence for the believer's life and fail to show how we are to situate ourselves in the world vis-à-vis those who suffer injustice.

---

[4] Pew Research Center, "The Religious Typology: A New Way e Categorize Americans by Religion" August 29, 2018. https://www.pewresearch.org/religion/2018/08/29/the-religious-typology. Accessed September 20, 2020.

[5] John Calvin, *Commentary on a Harmonies of the Gospels: Vol 3 Luke*. Edinburgh: Calvin Translation Society, 1846, 91.

Catholic Social Teaching

The Catholic presentation of the Gospel insists that salvation only comes through faithful participation in the Church[6] and its sacraments. When Protestants consider Roman Catholicism, they often think of the authority of the Pope, the veneration of Mary and the saints, and celebration of the Mass, Eucharist, and other sacraments, and many outside that tradition dismiss these as out of line with biblical faith. Yet, the tradition of Catholic social teaching, though not part of official doctrine, is rooted in a biblical understanding of God-imaged createdness that helps us appreciate the dignity and worth of every individual. These principles bolster our understanding of justice by first instructing us that all human life, from conception to death, is sacred and each person, regardless of race, ethnicity, ableness, economic standing, age, or any other attribute, is created in the image and likeness of God and is worthy of respect.

The principles of association and solidarity affirm the relationality of each person and call for a commitment to the common good of each while asserting that individuals have the right to participate in shaping their lives, society, and world and are not simply passive recipients of other's decisions.

In asserting God's preferential option for the poor and vulnerable, these teachings contend that God stands on the side of the most marginalized or oppressed persons and calls Christians to aid in their struggle. These teachings further contend that, as stewards of creation, we must respect the Creator by caring for the world's goods and making responsible decisions about the resources entrusted to us.

The subsidiarity principle leads us to render sufficient support to assist those in need without creating

---

[6] i.e., the Roman Catholic Church.

overdependence, increasing frustration, or fostering their hopelessness. Likewise, it understands the common good as a community being genuinely healthy and each person flourishing.[7]

Liberal Theology

By emphasizing or placing on par Christian ethics, the tradition of the Church, and the human experience of God over doctrine and Scriptural authority, liberal presentations of the Gospel attempt to communicate a faith that is considered reasonable, relevant, credible, and humane. However, Evangelical Christians critique this theology for its limited emphasis on personal holiness or lack of sanction on attitudes and behaviors Evangelical see the Bible holding as sinful.

Liberal presentations subordinate external sources of knowledge, such as Scripture, and represent them as inspirational rather than authoritative, seeing the autonomy of human reason or experience freeing us from coercive external controls over spiritual or ethical matters. Meanwhile, liberal presentations portray human nature as improvable, and are optimistic about a future in which humanity progresses toward ushering in the Kingdom of God and a more just world.

This theology has also been critiqued for linking the Gospel with what some perceive to be solely "political" causes considered beyond Scriptural purview of the mandate to prepare souls for eternity. Further, it is critiqued for replacing the delineation of Christian belief with participation

---

[7] See Charles E, Curran, *Catholic Social Teaching: 1891–Present*, Washington, DC: Georgetown University Press, 2002 or Thomas D Williams, *The World as it Could Be: Catholic Social Thought for a New Generation*, New York: Crossroad, 2014.

in the Church's work to establish God's moral-ethical Kingdom on Earth.

Yet we can't dismiss this theology as saying nothing to the renewal tradition, for it must be examined for its willingness to wrestle with how Scripture inspires us toward a more just world. It keeps before us important ideas about what it means to be relevant and of earthly good to this present generation.

A Renewal Understanding of the Gospel

An authentic renewalist Gospel presentation gleans from each of these traditions to present a holistic message that advances the Christian commitment to both personal and social holiness. Like the Evangelical presentation, it upholds the high authority of Scripture and its mandate for personal piety. At the same time, it notes the ethical implications of Catholic social teachings and the liberal understanding of working toward a more just society. Moreover, it gleans from the prosperity Gospel the expectation of empowerment of all men and women to live into God's already abundance that realization of the Kingdom makes available to us. Finally, it takes seriously liberal theology's attempt to advance God's Kingdom in this present world as a biblical mandate rather than the goal of a humanly inspired project.

The assertion that the Holy Spirit—the Spirit of the Living God—indwells believers in a vital way carries the obligation to demonstrate the difference such impartation makes. Understanding a biblical foundation for justice-seeking is equally important to the renewal heritage. Yet the more difficult question is whether such knowledge empowers the believer to act. For, we must answer John Richard Bryant's probing question, "Holy Spirit for what?" We must also be ready to answer his critique that ...[I]f all we are doing is jumping up and down in the air, speaking in other tongues, saying, "Yea, the Spirit is with us," that's fine. But... that is taking the gravy and leaving the meat.[8]

For as Bryant clearly lays out, the Spirit's outpouring on the believer has more substantial individual and corporate benefit for God's Church and for God's world than an individual experience. According to him,

> The meat of the Holy Spirit is for our... liberation and development [and] our strength as a people. And it has [always] been for that.[9]

His assessment reminds us that any grasp of Spirit-empowerment that does not engage issues of oppression or that causes the renewal community to disengage from justice-seeking is unscriptural and unsound. Any doctrinal system that doesn't consider the Spirit's liberative work and the real-world implications of Jesus' assertion that "I have come that you might have life, more abundantly" is inauthentic. The injunction to be holy as God is holy does not cast aside the requirement of a life sanctified from worldly indulgence, nor does it disregard the promise of eternal life in God's Kingdom where justice prevails. But it must properly include a fuller understanding of holiness that, as Paul admonishes, does not merely look out for one's own interests, but also the interests

---

[8] Quoted in Lawrence H. Mamiya, "A Social History of Bethel African Methodist Episcopal Church in Baltimore: The House of God and the Struggle for Freedom" in James P. Wind and James W. Lewis, eds., *American Congregations, Volume 1: Portraits of Twelve Religious Communities.* Chicago: University of Chicago Press, 1994, 266.

[9] Ibid.

of others.[10] It has as its mission the promulgation of that abundant life for all people in the here and now.

Spirit-empowerment enables us to envision the parameters of God's Kingdom as a community working toward the full participation of every believer in the temporal, as well as, eternal blessing of God. It doesn't understand eternal life as something grasped only in the hereafter, but as a reality each can seize in the here and now. It is inappropriate then to expect some believers to live in oppressive subsistence so that they may apprehend their justice in the far-off by-and-by, while others live in luxury."

Yet, too often, the renewal community takes its cues from fundamentalist factions that disregard any need to pursue justice and see any effort toward such a goal as unbiblical. In wrestling with the legitimate need to refrain from what Scripture identifies as sin—the deeds of the flesh—we jettison the equal concern of Scripture for justice-seeking.

Renewal Responses to Injustice

At the beginning of the contemporary renewal movement, William Seymour insisted that "a more sure sign" of Spirit-empowerment "… was love."[11] He was addressing the fact that for him, speaking in tongues, a sine qua non for many renewalists, was not, alone, a signal of whether one had received the baptism of the Holy Spirit. In the earliest days of this dynamic movement, Seymour attempted to demonstrate an equalitarian, classless, interracial vision of the Kingdom. Like Bryant, he understood there was a greater benefit, believing the Spirit had been imparted in great measure

---

[10] Philippians 2:4.
[11] William J. Seymour, "Doctrines," in William J. Seymour *The Doctrines and Discipline of the Azusa Street Apostolic Faith Mission of Los Angeles, California*, ed. Larry Martin. Joplin, MO: Christian Life Books, 2000, 42-3.

expressly to bring racial, gender, and class unity to the body of Christ as a witness to the broader society. By the end of his life, however, he was disappointed by what George McKinney called, "the tragedy of the missed opportunities of Azusa" [12] McKinney recounted that at Azusa Street,

> the liberating power of the Holy Spirit was manifested... The economically and socially depressed were set free. Racists were set free... Women were set free... the liberating power of God's presence... manifested itself in gathering people from all races and ethnic groups...[13]

Further, McKinney contended,

> ... God did something powerful at the Azusa Revival. During an era when racism, sexism and classism were accepted as normal, the Azusa Revival welcomed all races, classes and sexes as equals in the fellowship. Blacks, Whites, Asians, Hispanics and other groups were represented... welcomed under the same roof...[14]

Hans Baer and Merrill Singer's critique of religious communities' responses to injustice helps us understand how the missed opportunity of early Pentecostalism reflects historical responses of religious movements. They identify

---

[12] George G. McKinney, *The Azusa Street Revival Revisited*. A lecture presented at Beeson Divinity School, Sanford University in Birmingham, Alabama on October 3, 2001.

[13] Ibid.

[14] Ibid.

three types of responses—accommodation, reform, or activism.[15] The legitimacy of each is tempered by a faith community's worldview. Accommodationist responses focus on assisting the oppressed community in making the best of their unjust condition but do little or nothing to materially change it. Reform strategies help those with the injured community make themselves more acceptable. Activist strategies seek to disrupt the injustice, alter systems that bring about the crisis, and question crisis-forming elements. Each of these responses have been employed more or less effectively, in segments of the renewal community.

Accommodation

These responses call victims to settle for things as they are and resign themselves to the present reality and the hopelessness of bringing about a fair resolution. They offer spiritual solace while assisting the community in making the best of its condition. Such responses express a quietist

---

[15] A number of scholars employ this typology within various contexts. Among them are Hans Baer and Merrill Singer, *African-American Religion in the Twentieth Century: Varieties of Protest and Accommodation.* Knoxville: University of Tennessee Press, 1997; Adam Fairclough, *Better Day Coming: Blacks and Equality, 1890-2000.* New York: Viking Press, 2001; Julie Winch, *Philadelphia's Black Elite: Activism, Accommodation, and the Struggle for Autonomy, 1787-1848,* Philadelphia: Temple University Press, 1988; Barbara J. Harris and Jo Ann McNamara, "Women and the Structure of Society: Selected Research From The Fifth Berkshire Conference on the History of Women, Durham, NC: Duke University Press, 1984; Stephanie Yvette Felix, "African American Women in Social Reform, Welfare, and Activism: Southeast Settlement House, Washington, D.C., 1950-1970 Thesis" (M.A.)—University of Wisconsin—Madison, 1992; Ellen Carol DuBois "The Radicalism of the Woman Suffrage Movement: Notes Toward the Reconstruction of Nineteenth-Century Feminism" *Feminist Studies* 3:1/2 (Autumn, 1975), 63-71; and Joan Tronto "Changing Goals and Changing Strategies: Varieties of Women's Political Activities" in Claire Goldberg Moses and Heidi I. Hartmann, eds., *U.S Women in Struggle: A Feminist Studies Anthology*, Urbana: University of Illinois Press 1995.

passivity that suppresses human efforts to redress injustice in favor of waiting for future divine intervention and recompense. They are generally adopted by those employing otherworldly, revivalist religious expressions. Holding little confidence of remedying their situation, they interpret distress as a cross to be patiently borne in the temporal world while looking for reversal in the hereafter when God will overturn all oppression, and liberate all things.

Scriptural passages are read, repeated, and memorized regarding future deliverance. Even passages that deal with real lived situations such as Israel's deliverance from Egyptian captivity are recast in a spiritualized light. Sermons offer future deliverance both to the victim and the victimizer. The injured are assured that things will not always be this way: sufferers will, one day, in the eternal future flourish in the presence of a loving God. At the same time, generations of oppressors are relieved of complicity and assured that their prospering while others languish is, at least in part, due to that loving God's providential plan.

Songs remind the distressed that in the "sweet bye-and-bye," there will be another reality. They will have "golden slippers" to replace their threadbare shoes. They will freely walk on "streets of gold" with no lack or threat to their wellbeing. Their substandard housing will be traded for a mansion "just over the hilltop." They are comforted with the distant hope that one day they will have "two wings to fly away" where "the world can't do no harm."

Prayers are not for empowerment to fight oppression. Nor are they for retribution. Rather, these are prayers for the ability to patiently bear this "light [temporal] affliction." These supplications are to be able to forgive and love the oppressive renderers of injustice. Following the biblical prescription, they are for grace to *"love your enemies, do good to those who hate you, bless those who curse you, pray for those who are abusive to you.*[16]

These Scripture readings, sermons, songs, and prayers are not problematic within themselves, for they convey the Christian hope for ultimate restoration of all of Creation, when the already existing Kingdom is fully manifested and oppression ends. They anticipate that redeemed men and women will partake in God's intended covenant relationality. The danger, however, is in depicting this eternal future as the only future to which the oppressed can look forward. The problem is relegating any current remedy as irrelevant, unattainable, or sinful.

Accommodationist strategies include slave preachers exhorting hearers to content themselves with being slaves, using the Bible to convince them to dutifully obey masters and stay out of trouble.[17] These strategies said this is how it is supposed to be until Jesus returns. So oppressed slaves were urged to patiently make the best of their situation and not seek to be free. Indeed, these responses produce a false caricature of a God who is unconcerned and untouched by our mundane circumstances. They attempt to convince hearers that their crisis is God's will and might indeed be punishment for past behavior, eliciting a degree of self-pity or loathing by invoking the idea that, somehow, oppression is sanctioned by God or is the fault of the injured. Such accommodationist responses, which contend that the crisis must be humbly accepted, can paralyze and produce hopelessness or a false impression of acceptance within the oppressed community amid deep, unsettled, yet unspoken resentment.

---

[16] Luke 6:27b-28.
[17] See, for instance, Ephesians 6:5-6, Colossians 3:22, I Timothy 6:1, and Titus 2:9.

Or Accommodationism puts forth an understanding of a divine social order where various strata dutifully assume their place, bearing whatever that entails. It conveys the understanding that injustice carries a divine implication based on circumstances of birth such as race, gender, class, or even place that relegates individuals or communities to remain in distress or hope for little relief. These responses insinuate the fruitlessness of human attempts to alleviate injustice, further implying that if God desired a different situation, God "would make a way somehow," so all one can do is wait patiently on him.

Yet, accommodation responses are not always discernible. Often they simply involve inactivity, the failure to do anything at all. This acquiescence to the hopelessness of the situation is itself a strategy– albeit not a useful one. Failure to act is an act itself, for it facilitates the propagation of unrestrained injustice without the necessary resistance to constrain it. Accommodationist responses often cloak themselves as humility or an attempt to return a "biblical" answer. Yet a narrow view of what is biblical rejects almost any attempt at redressing harmful systems and vilifies any of the victims' attempts to assert their rights. Since human attempts at relief are couched as sinful, biblical warrant for bearing one's cross is invoked. Yet this is more than bearing persecution for faith's sake; it requires some good Christians to carry the cross of injustice, while other good Christians fair sumptuously, often at the victim's expense.

Such responses negate any attempt to deal with the consequences injustice foists on its victims as well as the possibility of genuine relief or liberation. God's supernatural intervention is the only opportunity for reprieve, hoped for against all odds. Moreover, it negates the reality that all men and women created in God's image deserve the respect and dignity due every carrier of the divine imprint.

Reform

Reform responses to injustice seek to integrate the injured community into the larger society in ways that are, at least minimally, acceptable, and least disturbing to the comfort of that society. While reform responses offer safe protest that doesn't change or eliminate these realities, sufferers accept, internalize, and incorporate the dominant community's values into their worldview. Further, while these responses offer limited critique, they never examine the underlying relationships–individual attitudes, habits, actions, policies and structures–that foster unjust outcomes. So, while some within the injured community are able to upgrade themselves to a predetermined level, reform responses hold little advantage and little hope of materially leveling the playing field to extricate the entire community. Those who succeed at reforming themselves become, at least nominally, more acceptable to the larger group. Yet, their individual success and achievement only highlight the unfairness of unjust systems for the majority of the oppressed community.

Profferers of reform solutions insist opportunity avails to anyone willing to take advantage of it. However, they fail to acknowledge the lack of equity built into self-perpetuating disadvantaging systems. Neither do they come to terms with the different impact of levels of disadvantage. They ignore the impossibility of pulling oneself up by the bootstraps, when historically denied access to means to acquire boots. Proponents quickly point to the few that make it as exceptions to the rule and bring up success stories of those who have excelled because of exceptional talents or through serendipitous circumstances. But they do not account for those who don't thrive. Moreover, they don't acknowledge that when individuals or communities elevate themselves, artificial ceilings based on preconceived assumptions limit how high they rise.

Within the civil rights context, for example, reform strategies include sermons on "racial uplift" that help some within the African-American community become more "refined," educated, and "socially acceptable." Such strategies allow a degree of autonomy and relative control for those meeting the prescribed criteria, if they don't threaten areas where the larger society has a substantial stake. Yet, if part of the community grows to the point that society's interest is threatened, the community may be supplanted.

Reform responses do not disrupt the broader community's sense of wellbeing. Instead, they place the onus on the injured individual or community to rid itself of unacceptable traits. And those who exhibit acceptable traits receive some privilege. These individualistic efforts mostly benefit those most able to align with the goals of the power class, distancing them from the broader victimized class and thwarting relief for the entire community. So those most able to render assistance are recognized for singular accomplishment and syphoned off for individual reward in ways that distance them from the rest of the community. This strategy convinces the ablest that, because of personal merit, they are different from the others. However, such tactics are precarious. Too often, as too many of the group approach the arbitrary standards, these standards are raised.

Often, those who wholeheartedly buy into reform ideology and rhetoric find it easy to buy into the worldview of the oppressive group. However, reformists are not really part of either world. They are never fully accepted by the oppressor, but don't feel comfortable with those of their community who remained trapped in the oppressive spiral.

Activism

Activist responses denote the vigorous, sustained effort to ameliorate injustice's cause and/or effect. They involve attempts to address issues by drawing attention to them and deliberately promoting correctives. These responses demonstrate that there is another way to be and challenge the socio-historical and theological premises on which crisis-forming systems rest. Further, they target the destruction of the foundations of these systems, making them of no effect.

For too many Christians, however, the words "activist" or "activism" evoke visions of militant protest, direct confrontation, violence, or revolution that seeks to uproot entire segments of society. This connotation prevents many who desire change from considering the activist option altogether. The thought that, as a believer, any activity might be misconstrued as fostering disruption to the community's peace prevents many from undertaking any steps that could reduce injustice.

Activist strategies, however, fall into two camps—strategic and radical—that in different ways, cover a full range of actions aimed at disarming unjust systems, and making them of no effect. Both attempt to bring about fundamental change that completely eliminates or greatly reduces the impact of not just the immediate crisis, but the entire crisis-forming system.

Strategic Activism

Strategic activism identifies essential elements of the crisis-forming system and methodically employs deliberate, tactical measures focused on creating substantive change.

This activism uses spiritual, political, social, economic, or other means to deconstruct these systems, first, educating or re-educating target audiences to make them aware of their working and then identifying means to eliminate or reduce their impact. Strategic activism may be private or public. Tactics include consciousness-raising, training, providing spiritual, economic, or material support to causes and institutions, political action and developing separate institutions to meet specific needs of a community. Private strategies informally attempt to convince individuals or communities of the need for justice and influence them to act. Public strategies formally focus on advancing the justice agenda in institutions such as legislatures, executive agencies, or courts.

The African American church engaged in strategic activism during the slavery and Jim Crow eras by establishing abolitionist organizations or newspapers to raise the consciousness of society regarding racial disparity. During the twentieth century, strategic activist responses included launching community education and economic empowerment efforts to address this disparity. Within the struggle for women's leadership in the Church, approaches include partitioning church leadership to authoring study resources to raise the consciousness of female and male church leaders.

Radical Activism

Radical activism employs measures considered quick and extreme (out of the purview of behavior expected within the larger context) to dramatically change or overturn crisis-forming systems and return the community to immediate wholeness. While most strategic activism happens behind the scene, radical activism is direct and visible. Strategies might include staging demonstrations, withholding material or financial support, forming coalitions, or establishing alternative movements that reject crisis-forming systems altogether.

Christian involvement in radical activism during slavery saw individual homes and congregations serving as Underground Railroad stations and Christians involving themselves in slave revolts. During the early twentieth-century temperance movement, women invaded saloons, broke up bars, and destroyed valuable liquor inventories. The marches, sit-ins, and boycotts that brought about civil rights legislation in the mid-twentieth century are examples of radical activism.

Renewalists rarely, if ever, employ radical activist strategies. But, Arthur Brazier's campaign to save his South Side Chicago neighborhood, Herbert Daughtry's battle for economic justice for black communities in Brooklyn, New York, and Frank Chikane's struggle against apartheid in South Africa serve as examples.[18] Perhaps, the Azusa Street Revival can be interpreted as radical activism as participants chose to obey God rather than man. Black, white, Latino/a brothers and sisters defied Jim Crow era racial norms to show the world another way to worship.

One of the worst labels one can acquire within the contemporary renewalist community is that you are radical. The very term carries with it connotations of some form of extremism. To denounce a stand or action as radical is to declare it unbiblical or ungodly, no matter how entrenched the injustice it addresses has become. Yet, the assessment of what is radical is often solely one of perspective. In any case, those committed to seeking justice cannot be deterred by

---

[18] For a more detailed discussion of each of their actions, see Chapter 6, "A Great Cloud of Witnesses."

words. Extreme, life-threatening injustice or oppression calls us to exert equally extreme yet, life-giving measures.

Renewal communities cannot assert they are entirely opposed to employing direct action tactics. Jesus overturning the money changers' tables is the clearest biblical example of this option.[19] Paul's demand that he be allowed to confront the Roman officials who had wrongly imprisoned him is another.[20]

Some within the renewal community assert that civil disobedience, as the deliberate violation of even unjust laws, is never warranted. In the last quarter of the twentieth century, however, fellow renewalists have joined other Evangelicals in using nonviolent protest such as abortion clinics sit-ins as a form of direct action. Others have use visible tactics to oppose legalization of gay marriage. Interestingly, these group could never lend that same level of support to securing voting rights or denouncing white supremacist groups.

On the other hand, progressive renewalist have successfully employed active nonviolence in numerous contexts. In some instances, they have vocally supported and worked for justice driven political candidates or run for office. At other times, they have engaged in civil disobedience including peaceful protests or refusal to obey unjust laws, orders or commands. But they have also more actively involved themselves in enterprises such as the operation of the Underground Railroad during slavery, raising conscientious objection to war, or harboring "illegal" immigrants.

At its core, Christian faith is, essentially, counter cultural and confrontational. It does not accept unbiblical cultural

---

[19] Matthew 21:12-13; Mark 11:15-18.
[20] Acts 16: 36-37.

rules as normal and confronts and subverts unjust or oppressive norms as outside the acceptable Christian witness. Cultural disobedience confronts and subverts dominant *cultural* norms to the point that it can ignite public dialogue about the rightness or wrongness of an issue, bringing societal change that is both profound and lasting. Jesus' conversation with the woman at the well was an act of cultural disobedience, as was Paul's insistence to his fellow Hebrew believers that in the new Christian community "there is neither Jew nor Greek,"[21] and the inclusion of women and the race mixing at Azusa Street during the radical Holiness and early Pentecostal eras.

Weapons of Our Warfare

While some may contend that "no form of "Christian activism" is truly Christian and all of it detours from the path the Church is to walk before the world and… leads to compromise and unholy alliances."[22] These critiques would also contend that… the Bible never advocates or contains an example of the involvement of God's people—within the Jewish community or the young Church—in political or social activism.[23]

Yet Scripture is replete with examples of activist stances taken by people of faith. The Hebrew midwives, Shiphrah and Puah, disobeyed Pharaoh's edict and spared the lives of the male babies, even lying to cover up their "rescue operation."[24] Moses approached Pharaoh to gain release of

---

[21] Galatians 3:28.
[22] Dave Hunt, "Christian Activism: Is It Biblical?" *The Berean Call*, November 1, 1989. https://www.thebereancall.org/content/christian-activism-it-biblical.
[23] Ibid.
[24] Exodus 1:15–21

the Jewish people from slavery is another.[25] Esther was willing to risk everything to save her people, declaring, "... I will go to the king, even though it is against the law. And if I perish, I perish."[26] By using her influence with the king to advocate for the Jews, she put her status as queen, and her life, on the line. And it worked. King Ahasuerus heard Esther's pleas and she and her people were saved.[27] In breaking religious and cultural rules, Jesus called into question the hypocrisy and unfairness of restrictions Jewish spiritual leaders imposed on the people.[28] Further, few examples of activism are as dramatic as the Lord's overturning of the tables and throwing the money changers out of the temple.[29]

For the Spirit-empowered Church, the renewed Christian, and their leaders, activism, rightly understood, is the only option. To remain silent, do nothing, and vilify those who actively seek redress is to stand on the side of oppression. The Apostle reminds us that as Spirit-empowered believers,

> ... the weapons of our warfare are not of the flesh, but divinely powerful for the destruction of fortresses. We are destroying arguments and all arrogance raised against the knowledge of God, and we are taking every thought captive to the obedience of Christ.[30]

As renewed, Spirit-empowered actors, we have at our disposal three God-given resources for successfully engaging

---

[25] Exodus 5:1-3.
[26] Esther 4:16.
[27] Esther 7.
[28] Matthew 23:13-15.
[29] Matthew 21:12-13; Mark 11:15-18.
[30] 2 Corinthians 10:4-5.

justice: pneumatological unction, pneumatological urgency, and prophetic audacity. To faithfully deliver an authentically liberating Gospel requires that these three elements are strategically and intricately intertwined and cannot be disentangled.

Pneumatological Unction

The imperative to actively seek justice cannot come from any external agenda, whether conservative, progressive, or liberal. Such motivation doesn't facilitate the sustained allegiance required to work toward lasting solutions. Secular agendas are changeable; they depend on the cultural norms, social context, or political realities on which they are founded, or which surround them. They are bound to various constituencies and loyalties, paying attention to the loudest voice in our ear at the moment, or the stage in life in which we find ourselves. These agendas go in and out of fashion so rapidly that even spiritual people can float from cause to cause or become disenchanted with the entire idea of justice-seeking.

The impetus for seeking justice must come from an entirely different place. A Spirit-driven sense of obligation to address the principalities and powers holding individuals and communities captive must exist within us. There must be an inner warrant to engage the forces that hamper human flourishing whether they stealthily hide within our religious circle or openly display themselves as identifiable outside forces. It must heighten our awareness such that the cry for liberation cannot be ignored or discounted. Further, it must tie us to God's project keeping in mind Paul's admonition to the Philippian church that "...with humility [we must] consider one another as more important than [our]selves;

[and] do not merely look out for your interests, but also for the interests of others. [31]

Pneumatological unction is God's investiture of authority on the Spirit-empowered believer to act as God's agent on behalf of sufferers of oppression within the so-loved world. Such unction implies that God's Spirit indwells, gifts, then sets apart, the renewed believer with a yoke-breaking anointing to announce the good news to the poor, the opening of blind eyes and prison doors, and setting free of those captive to so many unjust enslavements. Moreover, it prods us to acknowledge our obligation to fulfill this calling and mission.

The implication of the Spirit's indwelling carries with it a heavy responsibility. The injustice that grieves God's heart should grieve our hearts as well. Such unction should make us uncomfortable with any injustice, whether within our community or the world at large. As with the weeping prophet, Jeremiah, whose heart was breaking over the wickedness of his people even as he proclaimed God's impending judgment of the nation's sins,[32] our hearts should ache over injustice. When it does not, it is because we have accommodated ourselves to the world's systems. If injustice does not alarm us unless it lands at our feet, it is because we pay little attention to the Spirit's prompting as we go about our projects of self-aggrandizement.

Yet, we must speak hard truth in the genuine love of God. This often inconvenient and uncomfortable truth must consistently be voiced, even when it appears to fall on deaf ears and to remain unheard or unheeded. For our task is not to change the heart of the hearer(s); that is the Holy Spirit's sole prerogative. Our job is to keep the Spirit's agenda before

---

[31] Philippians 2:3b-4.
[32] Lamentations 2:11; 3:48.

those to whom it is addressed and confront them with the undeniable reality of situations of oppression.

If we open our spiritual eyes, the mantel accompanying the anointing causes us to see things others refuse to see and perceive truths that may escape others' sight. This unction causes concern about circumstances to which most give little attention, and to become uncomfortable around issues about which others find little dis-ease. It becomes the fire shut up in our bones such that we cannot keep quiet even when we desire to do so.

Though the passion—righteous indignation—of the Spirit-empowered justice seeker may be construed as raw anger, to disown this passion because of mistreatment, insult, or malice from another is to take the cause of justice lightly. Lackluster, half-hearted efforts do not upset, disturb, or make anyone uncomfortable, but also bring about no genuine change. For such change, by its very nature, is disquieting. Even for the bravest among us, change that is more than incremental is, itself, uncomfortable. Doing away with Christian passion ties our hands and renders us useless in helping to foment change. Instead, we settle for things as they are and simply ask, 'why.' Rather, what is needed are those who can envision a different way of living closer to the Kingdom and who dare ask, 'why not.'[33]

Our obligation does not rest solely on preaching God's word from the pulpit; or praying that somehow things will get better, it encompasses our whole life. We are "equipped for every good work"[34] because the power of God's Spirit accompanies our feeble efforts. Each Christian who honestly

---

[33] Robert F. Kennedy "Remarks at the University of Kansas, March 18, 1968." https://www.jfklibrary.org/learn/about-jfk/the-kennedy-family/robert-f-kennedy/robert-f-kennedy-speeches/remarks-at-the-university-of-kansas-march-18-1968. He was quoting George Bernard Shaw.

[34] 2 Timothy 3:17.

lays claim to the reality that it is the Spirit of the Lord—the Holy Spirit—that speaks and acts through us must take seriously what that requires. This claim is not to be taken lightly or frivolously employed on projects of self-fulfillment. Instead, those who claim that God's Spirit has been poured out in their hearts must also lay claim to a two-fold agency to act on behalf of God's Kingdom. It first involves an evangelistic unction that works to bring souls into that Kingdom. Yet, at the same time, judicial unction brings a burden against the oppression that opposes Kingdom rule.

Every renewed Christian carries in their soul an expression of the already-but-not-yet Kingdom "poured out within our hearts."[35] And that expression is to be then extended through us as love for God's world that enjoins our hearts to be grieved by the same conditions – hatred, violence, inequality, that grieves the heart of the God who is touched at every point by our human infirmity. So, situations that God detests should be equally detestable to us. Yet, we must do more than grieve. For the unction—the anointing manifested as the fullness of God—enables the yoke of oppression to be destroyed.[36] The word anointing means fatness, denoting our being excessively full of spiritual strength. Because we have been filled with God's Spirit, we have been strengthened to work on God's behalf and empowered to act on behalf of those within our communities and world who cannot act for themselves.

The book of Obadiah's harsh proclamation against the people of Edom reminds us we are responsible for our brother's wellbeing and cannot stand by and watch as those helpless victims are taken advantage of by powers bigger than themselves. Neither can we simply, as James' words

---

[35] Romans 5:5.
[36] Isaiah 10:27.

suggest, bid them God's speed while we do nothing to alleviate their suffering.[37]

The unction for justice is not an optional mantel to be put on or discarded at will, though it can be ignored amid the clamor for attention of seemingly good causes. Or, it can be relegated to those untapped, seldom-visited places in our spiritual closet that require too much of us. Though we pretend it is not there, it never goes away. Every time we bother to look in our spiritual mirror, it stares back at us, confronting us with the truth that the supernatural impartation of the Spirit has tagged us to involve ourselves in God's project. It pulls us toward engagement with the world that God-so-loved, reminding us that God has not given up on those for whom God was willing to send the Son to die, and neither can we.

In asserting access to such unction, we must refrain from the idolatrous hubris of assuming that we—and we alone—have the answer to the problem of injustice. We do not own the Holy Spirit. Instead, the Spirit owns us. We must not attempt to co-opt the Spirit for our benefit or to further our selfish agendas—to seek our prosperity, health, or wealth. That would certainly be idolatrous.

Yet, in our admitted weakness, strengthened by God's grace, we can only do our part, but each of us has a part to play. Certainly, injustice will not be eradicated until Christ ushers in His eschatological Kingdom. But that does not allow us to do nothing. Nor does it permit us to wait until flash points spring up to add our voice to a well-meaning, yet, ineffective chorus. The unction of the Spirit keeps justice seeking ever before us—if we are truly filled with God's Spirit, it is a part of who we are.

---

[37] James 2: 15-16.

Pneumatological Urgency

Without a sense of exigency, however, unction does little. Unused, wasted, idle power degenerates into inertia and atrophy, deadening our spiritual senses until we become unconcerned about anything that really matters. Or disuse leads to frustration. We sense something is wrong and somebody ought to do something, somebody ought to raise their voice to object. But not us!

Genuine unction brings about holy dissatisfaction—a deep uneasiness about the brokenness in this world that will not allow us to simply have a general feeling of discontent. Instead it should prompt us to do whatever we can and speak to whoever will listen. It aligns with God's heart and spurs us to take action to make concrete change.[38] Though this unction rests on every Spirit-empowered believer, for those who are called to lead, it carries an especially heavy responsibility for acquiring what is necessary to carry out their assigned task— it brings about a pneumatological urgency.

Pneumatological urgency convicts us that we are in a *now* moment. In every age, empowered believers whose ears are attuned to hear what the Spirt says to the Church carry within their souls a sense of immediate necessity. The Spirit impresses upon us the understanding that justice seeking cannot be put off until some more convenient time, but is a matter of life and death for the oppressed. Can't-wait issues require proximate attention because people die, families are destroyed and entire communities are devastated when we fail to act. The gravity of situations make justice seeking a priority and make us aware of the importance of addressing the need in the moment. This sense of urgency takes us

---

[38] See for example, Bill Hybels, *Holy Discontent: Fueling the Fire That Ignites Personal Vision*, Zondervan, 2007, and Frances Chan, "The Basis of Prophetic Preaching" in by Craig Brian Larson, Craig Larson, eds., *Prophetic Preaching*. Peabody, MA: Hendrickson Publishers, 2012.

beyond a propositional salvation that prioritizes correct confession while ignoring ethical demands of the Gospel. Here, again, Scripture clearly insists we are unfaithful when we assert love for God yet fail to care for others.

The Spirit directs our attention to critical areas of timely concern within our communities and world, shedding light on those that require our urgent attention. Jesus' exemplary prayer, "Your kingdom come; Your will be done on earth"[39] has significant impact for the justice project. First, it reminds us that it is God's Kingdom and will that we are seeking and not our selfish agenda. But importantly, we come to understand that it is here on earth, within our present reality, that we are to desire and work for it.

Each of us, individually and corporately, is responsible for ushering in that area of the Kingdom where God has situated us and within our circles of influence, as we, individually and collectively, intone the prayer, "Your Kingdom come," today, "on earth"—not only as it already is in heaven or in "the sweet by and by." Further, this pneumatologically driven sense of necessity precludes our passing the task of justice seeking to someone else. Rather, it alerts each renewed believer to the need to engage the opportunity for justice seeking wherever presents itself.

Yet, we cannot fool ourselves that passionate involvement will end injustice; we are not called to be God or bring about some unachievable utopia. Individual and communities' small, deliberate acts make a Kingdom difference in peoples' real lived situations. As with evangelism, where the impetus is not simply growing larger congregations but includes concern for individuals' eternal welfare, this spiritual imperative concerns itself with the holistic welfare of our communities.

---

[39] Matthew 6:10

Paul insists that when the urgency of God's love is not manifested in our encounters with the world, our supposedly Holy Spirit ramblings are no more than loud, unintelligible, and obnoxious noise.[40] These issues are not peripheral. Nor should they be dismissed as the dangerous work of social malcontents. For those living with dehumanizing oppression, these critical, life and death issues are matters of physical, material, emotional, and spiritual survival. They emanate from the heart of people who share a vital encounter with the "true and living God," and yet are impacted by the realities of this present world.

Every renewed believer should love justice, for Scripture is clear that it is impossible to love the unseen God while remaining unconcerned about the object of God's love. As brothers and sisters, created equally in God's image and sustained by God's grace, we have inherited a shared destiny. So ultimately, if we fail to address injustice, the threat to the Church or nation is not from outside enemies. Rather, left to fester unchecked, even unspoken, neglectful attitudes lead to a weak Church that faces self-destruction from within.

Any privately held, or publicly proclaimed, theology that does not enter into Jesus' project of announcing and pushing forward the possibility of abundant life within the already present manifestation of the Kingdom—while cognizant that its full presentation is only possible in the undetermined not yet—is impotent. For any individual or group that hides behind the Bible as an excuse to ignore the cause of justice, makes inauthentic use of the sacred text.

Justice issues take on new importance when viewed in light of the principles of the in-breaking Kingdom. For example, the issue of racial and ethnic justice becomes more than a secondary matter. In light of the Kingdom principle of

---

[40] I Corinthians 13:1.

the inherent dignity of each person created in God's image. It becomes crucial for restoring that dignity to make possible the thriving of communities of color that have been subjugated to discriminatory practices circumscribing every facet of their lives.

The promotion of the full humanity of women is critical when juxtaposed against the Kingdom principle of physical, emotional and spiritual wholeness for the entirety of God's creation. These efforts recognize that women's push for equitable treatment in the home, the Church and society goes far beyond any superficial attempt at gaining presumed "selfish" personal rights.[41] Rather, it relates to such heinous activities as sex trafficking, genital mutilation, spousal and partner abuse. The biblical narrative of God's pronouncement of Adam's dominance over Eve as a result of the Fall[42] is descriptive rather than prescriptive of God's desire for the human family. Misappropriating this text[43] is exemplified in locking women into abusive, loveless relationships which subject them to emotional, mental, and physical abuse or deny them any opportunity to employ particular God-given gifts outside of rigidly circumscribed, but cleverly theologically nuanced structures that sanction male privilege.

When viewed in light of the Kingdom principle of lack of want, work to engender economic wholeness, should be seen as ensuring the wellbeing of millions of individuals or entire communities forced to live at a subsistence level at the expense of the few who "fare sumptuously." This injustice has not only supported the institution of slavery in various

---

[41] See Susan C Hyatt, *In the spirit we're Equal: The Spirit, the Bible, and Women: A Revival Perspective.* Dallas, TX: Hyatt Press, 1998.

[42] Genesis 3:16.

[43] The same can be said regarding several Pauline texts that when taken out of their social context appear to prescribe the relegation of women to a second-class existence.

cultures, but has justified unfair labor laws, child labor, usury, and other forms of material oppression.

The cry for retributive justice challenges us to examine our legal systems against the Kingdom principle of fair judgment. Our effort in this area challenges authorized arrangements that unfairly target women, people of color, the poor, or members of other groups who cannot successfully navigate sanctioned structures. It requires that both those who are wrongfully detained or abused, as well as victims whose legitimate case is disallowed, get a fair hearing.

The motivation for the call for environmental justice becomes clearer when we understand the Kingdom principle that God did not leave the environment to fare on its own but enlists people, made in God's image, as emissaries responsible for the earth's care and preservation. It reminds us that we don't have the authority to abuse or misuse resources, and though the Fall began the earth's degradation, we are responsible for maintaining as much of its remaining integrity as possible.

The necessity of ensuring basic human rights to members of the LGBQT community gains new focus when viewed through the lens of the Kingdom principle of human liberation. While renewalists should not be forced to affirm cultural norms such as same-sex marriage, we must urgently love those with whom we vehemently disagree, extending them the same dignity and respect we crave. We don't have to affirm lifestyle choices, but must grant members of this community the right to live free of vilifying tirades that lead to hate. For, God so loved the world, not only those who we consider righteous according to our standards. So though we may not give credence to what we consider an unbiblical norm[44] or appear to sanction it, when we speak the truth to an issue, it must be in love. Renewalists who incite hatred and hate crimes toward homosexuals or those supporting abortion are unable or unwilling to hear a truly biblical call for love and who see themselves as God's duly authorized vigilante squad. They, themselves, are unbiblical.

While these issues exemplify the type of responses we are called to provide, they do not fully explore the desperate need of the quickly expanding global Pentecostal movement to come to terms with the myriad instances of injustice faced by those within the human family who are least able to fend for themselves. The social, emotional, and psychic cost of failure to appropriate a liberative understanding of Holy Spirit-empowerment has been the continuing existence of human slavery in a variety of forms throughout the globe. It forces entire races or cultures (including women and children) into dire poverty so that, at their expense, entire other races and cultures are not without the most trivial comfort—propped up by supposedly biblical, yet illusionary, sanctions such as manifest destiny and divine social order.

But what is not always as evident is the spiritual cost to the Kingdom that ensues from appropriating understandings that fail to marry personal and social holiness. For these misunderstandings leave communities immune to receiving an, allegedly, life-giving Gospel that offers no benefit for temporal flourishing. They esteem the offer of God's grace as bogus when it comes from a church passionately concerned about their eternal wellbeing but uninterested in advocating or ensuring their present survival. Therefore, we can't invite people to accept a Christ who cares little for their temporal

---

[44] Ben Giselbach, "The Bible Doesn't Say, 'Love the Sinner, Hate the Sin'" PlainSimpleFaith https://plainsimplefaith.com/the-bible-doesnt-say-love-the-sinner-hate-the-sin-the-defense-series/.

welfare and is *only* concerned with a spiritual good which can only be realized in the far-off future.

While religious platitudes often mask an unwillingness to tackle hard issues, pneumatological urgency does not settle for quick, pat answers. While such urgency wrestles tirelessly to find solutions, it has no patience with suggestions that "these things take time, especially when this response is a place-holder for inactivity or excuse for lack of engagement. It notes that the time for meaningful change is long overdue. Despite unrealized good intentions by well-meaning Christians, inaction propagates and maintains systems of oppression in which no, or little, alteration is accomplished over long periods. Those suffering injustice are admonished to be patient, for even they will have the benefits of crumbs that "trickle-down" from the master's table.

This urgency understands that patience is not always warranted and that there are times when patience, itself, can be deadly. There are situations in which not to speak out—not to contest injustice and oppression—costs lives. Still, we cannot labor over a grandiose vision of changing everything at once, knowing that the already Kingdom that exists in God's heart and mind has not yet fully unfolded in our earthly reality. Yet, the need of the moment calls for a response. When we are made aware of the toxic consequences of injustice, we must speak and act. Yet, everything around us, even within the religious context, constrains us to be quiet. For even in the community of faith, there are rewards for remaining silent and disincentives for prophetically addressing others' oppression.

Why should we care? Because God cares! Why should we burden ourselves? Because God is touched by our infirmities! Why should our spirit grieve? Because the Spirit broods over injustice!

Prophetic Audacity

All who embrace justice understand that bigotry from anyone, including leaders, is intolerable and should not be inflamed by careless, ill-considered words from those in authority. But, neither can such bigotry be ignored as if it did not matter. Instead, it must be called out for what it is and shut down before it can incite another generation to violence and fanaticism. The unction to engage injustice rests on every Spirit-empowered Christian, and many feel a sense of urgency to contend with these issues. Yet, only those possessing what my grandmother called "holy boldness"— willingness to risk the discomfort of prophetically speaking and acting—can fully embrace the justice-seeking task. It is not enough to be either prophetic or audacious. We must always keep the two qualities in tandem; there must always a partnership culminating in Prophetic Audacity.

The demonstration of prophetic audacity requires the spiritual boldness to carry out God's Kingdom project, not our own. This audacity attempts to promote God intentions for the so loved world with confident disregard for personal gain or advancement, conventional thought, or unjust restrictions.

Prophetic Passion without Audacity

Being prophetic without possessing audacity only leads to frustration with ourselves, the issue and those who cause injustice. We know God is speaking to the condition, but don't dare say anything. We don't want to stand out and be different. It is personally safer to go with the existing state of affairs and less threatening to fit into a secure corner and watch. Too often, even when progressive, prophetic Christians realize the seriousness of a situation, they remain silent when what is called for is a "fit word."

Yet, while the audacious must speak to injustice in society, we must also address injustice in our ranks—the Church and the broader faith community. We are called to confront those who name themselves Christians–dare to call themselves Spirit-empowered—when they attempt to use their perceived spiritual authority to lord over others. Since judgment... begin[s] with the household of God...[45] it begins first with us.

Old Testament prophets railed against infractions of God's justice among his chosen people. Amos denounced leaders taking advantage of the hard work of the poor, treating them with contempt, taking bribes[46] and rigging the scales and currency.[47] Micah attacked the "chiefs of the house of Israel" ...who eat the flesh of my people" and "build Zion with blood and Jerusalem with wrong."[48] Jeremiah was daring enough to tell the exiles, that they would not quickly return to their homeland despite the false predictions of more popular prophets.[49] Isaiah spoke for the God who denounced "the elders and princes of his people," who hold "the spoil of the poor is in [their] houses"[50] and extend their land holdings at the expense of others.[51]

The prophets spoke many pronouncements to less than receptive audiences regarding issues critical to the community's survival. These were life and death matters— injustices that needed to be righted; oppression that needed to cease. To say that it was uncomfortable for their hearers is a gross understatement, but these men still stood in their

---

[45] 1 Peter 4:17.
[46] Amos 5:11.
[47] Amos 8:5.
[48] Micah 3:3-10.
[49] Jeremiah 29:8-10.
[50] Isaiah 3:14.
[51] Isaiah 5:8.

prophetic anointing and declared God's heart and mind.. Then, as now, dire times call for such boldness. The issues facing the Church, our communities and our world call us to use our voices, influence, and actions to declare truth in places where it is not easily heard, if heard at all. It may demand that we offend sinful motivations that masquerade as spiritual agendas. It may require breaking ranks with those in our community to stand righteously indignant. Despite criticism from within our ranks, because Go's Spirit is upon us, we are called to stand unwaveringly on the side of the oppressed. We are called to be willing to risk offending members of our congregation, ministry colleagues, or denominational and spiritual leaders who oppose the cry for justice.

Paul's admonition to "be diligent to keep the unity of the Spirit, in the bond of peace"[52] is often heard as having to keep peace at any cost. So we tip-toe around vitally important matters declaring these conversations off limits. In doing so, these life-destroying issues are suppressed, lingering just below the surface of our spiritual skin and turning to hostility and self-hatred until the individual or community explodes in rage. Sometimes the immediate quiet of the moment must be broken; so that truth can be spoken and genuine unity can ensue.

Often we are silent, while just below the surface we are simmering with unresolved dissatisfaction or discontent. As the injustice is left unopposed it repeatedly slaps us in the face and irks us. But in the name of Christian quietism, we dare not make waves; we dare not discomfort our brother or sister. Yet for any genuine resolution to occur, authentic truth must be spoken in genuine love. Or myths are invented, excuses are created, and the longer the cycle of denial exists, the more entrenched the lie becomes.

---

[52] Ephesians 4:3.

Audacity Without Prophetic Passion

Any attempt at authentic prophetic audacity not driven by a passion for seeking justice, because we, like Jesus, are touched by others' infirmities, is ingenuine. Authentic audacity must never be hubris or silliness. Indeed, true prophetic audacity requires passionate humility that does not seek to bring attention to ourselves for the cause of self-aggrandizement, but only to bring attention to our just cause.

Audacity without prophetic passion is foolhardy and reckless. For prophetic audacity does not rush headlong into any contentious arena, but prayerfully weighs the cost of its involvement. While exercising spiritual confidence, it considers that the benefit is far greater than any social, economic or material lost that might be incurred, and is unafraid of the consequences of the task, for it sacrifices its own comfort for the wellbeing of those who dare not speak for themselves.

Such passion is not brashness for the sake of shock value. Neither does it adopt the Lone Ranger approach, as if any of us are the only vehicle through whom God acts in any situation. Instead, it willingly joins with others to bring about the desired end.

Again, audacity is not anger, though the passion that accompanies it is often mistaken as such. For the prophetically audacious Christian knows that since "our struggle is not against flesh and blood," it is futile to launch carnal attacks on individual entities. Instead, we battle against entrenched life-destroying systems that Scripture identifies as "the rulers, powers, world forces of this darkness," and "spiritual forces of wickedness in the heavenly places." This audacity, then, requires spiritual discernment to know the difference and fortitude for the long haul.[53]

---

[53] Ephesians 6:12.

Audacity must be provocative, but does not crudely stimulate anger or disgust. Rather, our audacious passion should, as Scripture implores, provoke others to good works,[54] stirring empathy for justice for sufferers of oppression and inspiring other's action on their behalf.

For the prophetically audacious, this provocation is intentional, for as the writer of the book of Hebrews also admonishes us, we are to consider how to provoke or encourage one another to love.[55] What we say and do should move those in our circles of influence to be uncomfortable with injustice.

Again, provocative measures don't aim at insighting our hearers to become defensive or more entrenched. Rather, we intend to push for more genuine responses to the real harm of injustice, make them uncomfortable with safe answers. For finally, this disturbing, Spirit-driven passion will not let us leave, the so-called, well enough alone. It cries out, Enough!

What Shall We Say Then?

When, as prophetic renewalists, we lay claim to these the tools of pneumatological unction, pneumatological urgency and prophetic audacity we are insisting that our movement is the contemporary fulfillment of Joel's prophecy that "... *in the last days, the sons and daughter upon whom God's Spirit rest will prophesy.*" Moreover, we legitimize the claim that these sons and daughters will boldly speak truth, understanding that silence is not a comfortable option. For political correctness is itself a loaded tactic to keep at bay any substantive critique of engrained injustice. Further, while indiscriminating individuals see any language that attempts to disarm unjust attitudes as politically incorrect, uncritical,

---

[54] Hebrews 10:24.
[55] Hebrews 11:23 (NKJ21).

offhanded language about historically loaded subjects only extends oppression.

Prophetic renewalists do not bristle at being labeled "radical," realizing that Scripture is radically wedded to justice, and anything less than such a commitment falls short of the biblical mandate. Apprehension about having our language dismissed as politically correct cannot excuse failure to address vital issues, for "God has not given us a spirit of timidity, but of power and love and discipline."[56] Again, empowered believers can join with Christ to claim, "the Spirit of the Lord is upon me," as an extension of his ongoing work in the present age. To stake this claim, however, means willingly partaking in the implications of the Cross, dying to our self-interest, and taking on the fellowship of his sufferings.[57]

Prominent Baptist pastor and Christian leader, Claude Alexander insists that the contemporary Church needs "a muscular body of Christ [that] cannot avoid or ignore harsh realities…" but "finds courage to look at those realities for what they are and allow the strength of the God of justice, mercy, grace, love, and peace to equip us to come together."[58] While Alexander speaks expressly to the realities of racial injustice, the issues of male dominance and misogyny, systematically induced poverty and economic disparity, human trafficking, and homophobia that fosters hatred and violence toward those in the LGBQT community are no less compelling. The struggle is finding the courage to stand for

---

[56] 2 Timothy 1:7.
[57] Philippians 3:10.
[58] Cited in Kyle Rohane, "Ministry after a Fatal Police Shooting" *Christianity Today* Oct 3, 2016. https://www.christianitytoday.com/pastors/2016/october-web-exclusives/ministry-after-fatal-police-shooting.html Bishop Claude Richard Alexander, Jr. is Senior Pastor of The Park Church in Charlotte, North Carolina.

what renewalists see as biblical values regarding the dignity and worth of every human being. Since "all have sinned and come short of the glory of God," every person deserves to be treated with the dignity and respect accrued to them because of their indelible God-imaged createdness.[59]

In the end, no single individual is called to transform the entire society or overthrow all oppression, and it is foolish to hope to do so. Rather, each is called to speak and act for Kingdom principles in such a way that these principles are clearly visible to our context as the possibility of another way to be. We are called to stand with and speak alongside those who are considered least as they struggle to be heard. We are called to make just decisions in our spheres of influence that cause those within those orbs to see, think, speak, and act more justly.

The convergence of unction, urgency and audacity allows the prophetic voice to wrestle with and call out issues when it would be easier to leave them alone. It invites us to come and die, for if there is nothing for which I am willing to die (figuratively or literally), then I have not really lived. Death comes in many flavors. Though we will all face physical demise at some point, we must be willing to die to personal agendas and ambitions; we must be willing to die to fear of rejection for doing what is right. As important, however, we, personally, must be willing to die to behaviors that bring about injustice.

Dealing with Hard Issues

As Stanley Grenz suggests, "[o]ur Christian concern is to acknowledge every person as the recipient of God's

---

[59] For a full discussion of this concept, see Stanley Grenz, *Welcoming But Not Affirming An Evangelical Response to Homosexuality*. Louisville, KY: Westminster John Knox Press, 1998.

compassion, concern and love."[60] Yet, the renewalist imperative to hold Scripture in high authority produces a measure of angst and inner tension as we sometimes wrestle with seemingly incongruous positions on matters of moral concern. While renewalists should not be expected to jettison biblical convictions regarding what they see as non-negotiable scriptural sanctions on highly contested issues,[61] we cannot weaponize Scripture to vilify those who do not support our posture. Scripture, and the love of God should always be instruments that draw people to examine truth together rather than means of spreading hatred.

Following Christ's example, we are compelled to treat each person (including those with whom we vehemently disagree) with genuine love. Truly abhorring attitudes and action we hold to be sinful, but showing God's love to those who hold such attitudes and engage such actions requires us to first acknowledge our own unrighteousness. Contemporary issues such as a woman's right to choose to abort a fetus or the "civil rights" to which the LGBQT community lays legal claim, present a challenge to renewalist. Still, there are certain human rights that each man and woman (no matter how they identify themselves) hold: to live without fear of violence, to be able to earn a living, and to receive adequate medical care. To oppose these basic rights is to oppose justice.

At the same time, we must question our attitude toward those who show racial bias or bigotry, uphold misogynist attitudes or show a consistent lack of concern for justice. If we

---

[60] Stanley J. Grenz, *Welcoming but Not Affirming: An Evangelical Response to Homosexuality*. Philadelphia: Westminster John Knox Press, 1998, 156.

[61] Such as homosexuality, abortion, or marital fidelity.

are not prayerful, our response to them can easily degenerate into self-righteous vilification.

Grenz's assessment that while the [renewal] Church's response to homosexuality cannot be affirming, [but] must always be a welcoming community,[62] is on target. Anything less would be injustice. More importantly, we must be able to articulate what we hold to be a biblical position without resorting to mean-spiritedness. Adopting a different lifestyle does not make a person less human or deserving of God's love. So, our attitude, speech, or actions should never strip a person of their humanity or the dignity due them as created in God's imaged. But such a response is hard to pull off and requires prayerful and thoughtful recrafting of previously "acceptable" ways of dealing with these issues.

Whether it is legal or not, the issue of a woman's "right" to choose abortion is another difficult issue. Renewalists who hold Scripture in high authority have every right to consider aborting of a viable fetus, for the simple "expediency" or doing away with a "surprise" or inconvenient pregnancy as murder. Yet, the issue is much more complex than Christians on both side would claim and requires a solid biblically supported, yet compassionate, response.

The Bible declares that God forms human beings inside a mother's womb,[63] and before we are born God intimately knows us.[64] So renewalist are right in their conviction that all human life is precious to God[65] and must be protected and defended. An inconsistency exists, however, when Christians hold violence against the fetus as unbiblical while considering violence against abortionist as, somehow, God

---

[62] Hence the title of the work.
[63] Psalm 139: 13-16.
[64] Galatians 1:15.
[65] Isaiah 43:1-2.

ordained. We are also inconsistent to insist on the ultimate value of the life of the unborn unless we are willing to actively reach out women facing difficult circumstances and present them with authentic alternatives.

The Christian community has sometimes shown itself to be passionate about the issue of abortion yet indifference to consideration extenuating circumstances rape, incest (especially involving minor girls), or mental incapacity in which these women find themselves. The lack of communal, economic, and social support often coerce an abortion that would not be necessary in a more just society.[66] Dangerously, many women who lack access to a legal abortion services suffer irreparable physical harm, emotional scarring, or spiritual damage or die when they resort to back-alley options.[67] Yet, the Christian community is often complicit in driving women to think of abortion as the only answer to an unwanted pregnancy.

In either the case of our response to the LGBTQ community or the abortion issue, renewal faith communities often fail to provide safe places to consider their complexity. Unlike Jesus response to the sinners with whom he came into contact, frequently, our pronouncements have been vilifying rather than compassionate. For just as frequently, we have hated the sinner as much as the sin and have been unwilling to concede or own impiousness. Moreover renewalist have sometimes relegated the severity of these "personal" sinfulness as more damning that the sum total of bigotry, atrocity and evil foisted on others. Where renewalists have failed to craft authentically loving responses to hard issues,

---

[66] Religious Institute, "Abortion: Providing an Alternative" http://religiousinstitute.org/denom_statements/abortion-providing-an-alternative/.

[67] Most or many of this would be borne by women in lower socio-economic classes, including women of color.

the void invites a cacophony of deafeningly confusing voices of those seizing the opportunity to spew hatred, while cries for justice from those experiencing unchecked bigotry remain unheeded.

Prophetic audacity does not hide from hard issues; instead, it seizes the opportunity to speak truth to the void. Further, however, our community must be willing to turn the spotlight on itself. Failing to speak prophetically, the renewal community has cultivated a generation that rejects a faith that is unconcerned about injustice and oppression. Legalism, excessive materialism, misogynist ideas, and hateful homophobic attitudes and gestures have driven them to go after alternative religions or reject God altogether, seeing secular means or the courts as the only avenues for bringing about real change. Some past endeavors wrongly imposed Western standards of civility as biblical righteousness and used cultural norms to scapegoat a failure to confront unethical, life-threatening, and dehumanizing practices. What is required is a theological turn toward the prophetic to save the physical, emotional, psychic and spiritual lives of our sisters who cannot fend for themselves.

Abdicating our role as the moral conscience of society and remaining silent on issues of systemic racism, human indignity, and government misconduct, allots no room for complaint when others apply secular solutions. Further, as society's moral and spiritual conscience, Christians must promote the public good by actively opposing any system that inhibits every person's opportunity for flourishing.[68] When we stand together we withstand the onslaught of those who work at subverting human flourishing. Or alternatively,

---

[68] RaShan Frost, "Christian Activism and Reform in the Age of Black Lives Matter" *Providence Magazine,* June 11, 2020. https://providencemag.com/2020/06/christian-activism-reform-age-black-lives-matter.

when we fail to do so, we fall prey to disruption of the justice-seeking project as its enemies employ the anarchy of disunity to wreak havoc.

Conclusion

Pneumatological unction calls us to deliberately involve ourselves in God's project of making the so-loved world more just. We are not called to create a pre-fall utopia. Yet we are made aware through the Spirit's empowerment that we can make our circle of influence more representative of the not-yet Kingdom.

Pneumatological urgency alerts us that too much is at stake! It informs us that the vision for our children to live in a better, though imperfect, world will not unfold of its own accord. Instead, as stakeholders, each of us must emphatically denounce and vigilantly work to destroy all forms of repulsive, menacing bigotry, with all the unction, urgency, and audacity deposited in us by the Spirit.

Prophetic audacity places us front and center—face to face—with the real issues of life, the weightier matters of the Law. For Jesus reminds us that more important than religiously observing ritual is the observance of kindness. It is what truly matters in the economy of the Kingdom.

To fail to come to terms with the goal of liberation is to fail to restore the full clarity of the image of God within every person so that their worth may be estimated in light of God's word. It is to abdicate our claim to be Spirit-empowered. Certainly, the central focus of renewal spirituality and proclamation is the offer of eternal life through the appropriation of the atoning work of Christ. But, that offer is not couched in a pie-in-the-sky, white robe and golden slipper escapism. Instead, at times, that offer has to be more broadly expressed as socially, as well as spiritually, liberative. The personal implications of Jesus' offer of abundant life in the here and now, extrapolates to liberation for oppressed persons and communities.

Therefore, it is problematic to mistake the theological conservativism of most renewalists' for socio-political accommodation. Indeed, theological conservatism, the penchant to engage the Scripture as authoritative warrant for all of God imaged humanity's access to abundant life, should drive the socio-political agenda. While renewal rhetoric rarely employs explicit socio-liberative language, it must communicate that the experience of Spirit empowerment has implications beyond ecstatic expression in worship or personal piety. It must convey the truth that the God who so powerfully visited and invested God's self in us, is concerned with temporal reality of the oppressed. In the renewal experience, we can find what Ithiel Clemmons defines as a "spirituality of deliverance"[69]

George McKinney's critique of the missed opportunity heirs of the Azusa Street Revival to envision a liberative spirituality convicts renewal leaders that we often fall short. He invoked that vision in calling upon those within the movement to,

> mustered the courage of Martin Luther, Dietrich Bonhoeffer, Martin Niemuller, and Martin Luther King, and declare to the powers that -..., "We are brothers and sisters... in covenant, we will not be separated by your laws. [As the] members of the family of God... [w]e will worship, minister, and

---

[69] Ithiel Clemmons, *Bishop C.H. Mason and the roots of the Church of God in Christ.* Lanham, MD: Pneumalife Publishers, 1997, 68.

fellowship together…, go to jail together, or… die together… so help us God…"⁷⁰

McKinney insisted that such a position would have resulted in lynchings and martyrdom, but God's truth would have won in the end and the Civil Rights Movement would have been fought on spiritual grounds and the church would have fulfilled Christ's mandate to be salt in a tasteless society and light in that darkness…⁷¹ His challenge to the renewal community still rings true today:

> it is time to prayerfully consider the next step to realize the vision of unity and justice which was only beginning when it was aborted [at the end of the Azusa street revival].⁷²

As "critical reconcilers," Christians must continuously critique what is wrong or unjust at while working to show a different way to be in relationship with the other. As we name ourselves Spirit-empowered, we have identified ourselves as having the tools to bring about change. The mantle of pneumatological unction, our sense of pneumatological urgency, and our claim to prophetic audacity equip us for that. But we must choose whether to employ them on behalf of God's project or allow them to lie dormant as we critique and complain about the rhetoric and actions or others.

---

[70] McKinney, *The Azusa Street Revival Revisited*.
[71] Ibid.
[72] Ibid.

8

Conclusion

In every age and within every context, those who name themselves as God's people have stood on opposing sides of issues of justice, declaring both the righteousness of their cause and their allegiance to God. For some observers, the confusion that this causes is reason enough to abandon efforts to seek justice. But for the empowered believer, it can never justify leaving the status quo of injustice in place. Too many lives are at stake, and disengagement compromises our Christin witness of a loving God who cares for and desires the wellbeing and flourishing of all humanity.

The realities that threaten lives of individuals within communities as well as the lives of entire communities are too critical to ignore. Yet, the renewal tradition's approach has often been to obscure these realities and accommodate the oppressed to a liminal, quasi-spiritual state in which they feel close to God but are un-relieved of their distress. Or, the movement seeks to reform the excluded members of society to render them more acceptable and therefore more worthy of inclusion. These approaches limit the Spirit's ongoing work in forming the Church for contemporary ministry and fail to address the root causes of oppression. On the other hand, renewalist have been reluctant to adopt solutions that they see as negating the authority of Scripture in guiding Christian practice and allowing attitudes that embrace unbiblical agendas and lifestyles.

Ongoing biblical activism aligned with the renewal heritage of a "great cloud of witnesses" that have continued to affirm the Lordship and atoning work of Christ while demonstrating His compassionate concern for the oppressed.[1] These women and men refused to settle for a Christian faith totally focused on other worldly affairs. Their work incorporates pneumatological unction that speaks of the gravity of these matters, pneumatological urgency that prods expedient action, and prophetic audacity that makes justice seeking a provocative priority.

Jesus' message is never either-or—salvation or justice; it is always both-and. Through His atoning work on the cross, He offers eternal redemption to every person. Yet, His temple declaration that "the Spirit of the Lord is upon me" offers every believer the opportunity to extend the gospel—the good news of the inbreaking of the Kingdom—not only to the spiritually poor, but to those lacking the material resources to sustain themselves or are dispossessed of the dignity and respect due them as God-imaged humanity. God's proclamation of release is as much from captive systems as it is to the captivity of sin. The offer of recovery of sight is both for spiritual blindness and those blinded by the deceitfulness of dehumanizing lies. He came to set free those who are oppressed—tormented–by sin as well as those who are oppressed—tormented–by sinful systems and by others' sinful actions.

Rigid labels, such as right or left, conservative or liberal, and even Bible believer or simple Jesus follower, seek to define some as involved in justice seeking and others as uninterested. But these identifications obscure the reality that justice is rooted in the very character and nature of God. For Scripture reminds us that "all God's ways are justice" and God is always "faithful, without iniquity, just and upright."[2] The building blocks of justice, therefore, lie in acknowledging

---

[1] This was originally posted on William Seymour College's blog.
[2] Deuteronomy 32:4.

that human dignity, flourishing, and the sacredness of life stem from recognizing the God-imaged createdness in each person and understanding justice as a central component of God's perfect righteousness, undying mercy, and radical love.

Justice-seeking creates Kingdom space for every God-imaged person in the temporal here and now, giving witness to the ultimate eternal justice yet to come. Therefore, every time we use our voice, influence, or actions in justice's behalf, we foreshadow that coming Kingdom. Still, challenges to misogyny; human trafficking; child, spousal, or elder abuse; economic exploitation; human rights violations; high infant mortality rates; racial and ethnic prejudice; and other injustices inevitably lead to conflict, especially when they seek to change "systems."[3] Since the renewal community often has difficulty relating evangelism and such justice efforts, we've got a long way to go in wrestling with how to announce the good news of God's Kingdom that is both proclaimed and lived out in a convincing manner.

Importantly, however, the Holy Spirit has been poured out for both our spiritual and intellectual empowerment, and is not only concerned with the liberation of our soul, but also with our minds to work for the materially poor, and those blinded by, and captive to, oppression by very real political and social principalities of this world. Intellectual empowerment starts with educating ourselves about issues of injustice, for Scripture's admonition that *"my people are destroyed for lack of knowledge,"*[4] is not simply concerned with knowledge about God, but also about God's ways with the world.

---

[3] World Vision, "What does Social Justice Really Mean?" https://www.worldvision.org/blog/social-justice-really-mean. Accessed January 15, 2020.

[4] Hosea 4:6.

We must first admit what we don't know. Becoming literate regarding justice overcomes the senseless, harmful bifurcation between biblical and social justice as, again, we come to understand that "all God's ways are [always] just." By starting with what we see in our community and relating to their real world struggles, we are able to humanize injustice in ways that help us break out of partisan political frameworks, examine presuppositions about people and issues, and acquire knowledge that engenders empathy.

Consciousness-Raising

Once we are enlightened about the biblical nature of justice-seeking, we cannot assume that others recognize it. Believers can easily become comfortable with their situations, convinced that everyone else who desires to can fare as well.. We tell ourselves that those who need to know about injustice are already aware, but, in reality, even many Christians are conveniently oblivious to the injustice that is part of the fabric of societies. Consciousness-raising is simply aiding people to see beyond themselves, their self-interest, and their world. We alert them that not imagined, but actual, issues effect real people with real, often unintended consequences. Further we show that there might be real solutions in which we can participate.

Consciousness-raising happens in many ways. When we intentionally hold people and institutions accountable for creating, implementing, and sustaining policies and practices geared toward society's flourishing we demonstrate to others that such action is possible. When we incorporate the prophetic and spiritual into our advocacy we help the Christian community to embrace justice-seeking as something in which they should be involved. When we include justice in our preaching, corporate prayer, and study of God's word, we move the issue beyond being solely a secular matter of personal choice to a spiritual mandate. When we support, encourage, and lift up other justice seekers and join with them in small efforts, we show that even this investment can make a difference. Refusing to participate in unjust conversations and actions, and saying why we are absenting ourselves is an act of consciousness-raising. So we are not just failing to show up, but letting others know that what they are doing is harmful.

As an exercise of faith, we can begin by praying that justice is done in the communities and world in which we live. Yet the Bible is clear that "faith without works is dead." So where do we begin? Since the Church is, first, the body of Christ and a living organism, those who are oppressed within its borders are calling the rest of the body to start here. Whatever we seek to accomplish must be guided by the word of God, the guidance of the Holy Spirit, and sustained prayer. The Church's primary purpose—the reason for its existence and our being Christian—is to worship God and represent God in the earth. Believers, therefore, must always be mindful that truly spiritual worship must be accompanied by a true representation of a God who does not hate, is never unfair or unjust, does not discriminate based on arbitrary characteristics, or sign on to hidden agendas not aligned with God's nature.

For, as Paul reminds us, when any part of the Christian body suffers we are all in pain. The same is true with the human family. If any member of that family is distressed—especially when we say or do nothing to help—we are all a little less human. Further, we carry a sense of guilt, and live with the fear of retaliation, or of having to trade places with the oppressed, knowing that but for God's grace and the circumstance of birth we could be in their position.

The most audacious form of activism is uncompromisingly speaking truth, in love, to power. It is willingness to unashamedly express a clear word that calls out all forms of injustice for what they are while addressing hearers within Christ's Church as brothers and sisters. To call into question those un-Christlike actions may require breaking ranks with some in our own communities. Despite criticism from within, audacity allows us to not back down and stand unwaveringly on the side of those experiencing injustice

Seeing the justice-seeking project through to the end requires tenacity to stand for the long haul. This tenacity first asks us to speak small truths, take small actions, and celebrate each small victory, realizing that the struggle is unending. Yet, our involvement must grow as we become more spiritually vital. We can never be satisfied with seeking less than full justice, though we know that it will not be realized this side of the not-yet Kingdom.

We begin justice-seeking by supporting from behind before stepping out front. We can align with people who are doing justice and who are looking for those to participate with them in some small way. Measures such as supporting letter writing campaigns, calling legislators, or attending meetings of local agencies are useful. Joining with other organizations—often with very different motivations, beliefs and constituencies—does not sign off on their entire agenda. Instead, strategic work on clearly defined, common goals brings collective political strength or influence that yield greater results than we might imagine. These efforts allow renewalist to marry biblical faith, and appreciation for the Spirit's work in Church and individual with a mandate for practical justice-seeking. For, ultimately our hope is to convey a prophetic witness grounded in a biblical understanding of

Spirit-empowered justice-seeking using our voice, influence and actions.

Voice

The book of Ecclesiastes tells us that as well as a "time to keep silence," there is "a time to speak." Knowing when to speak and when to be silent requires as much wisdom as knowing what, how and to whom to speak. As Spirit-empowered leaders, we have choices. Our voice can be either a tool that speaks for those who cannot speak for themselves, or a weapon for stirring injustice. Yet silence—not to speak when it is needed—is as much a weapon. For it is true that often, all that is necessary for injustice to prevail and "for evil to triumph is for good men [and women] to [say] nothing."[5] Frustrating muteness from the tradition signals culpability and complicity. Maintaining silence hints at acquiescence to the status quo while Scripture enjoins us to,

Open your mouth for the mute,
For the rights of all the unfortunate.
Open your mouth, judge righteously,
And defend the rights of the afflicted and needy.[6]

As advocates, our task is not solely to speak for the oppressed, but to assist individuals or groups to find and effectively use their own voice. For we don't assume we have the answer for what others need; but trust that they know, or can help them identify and articulate, where they have been harmed, what they have been denied and the degree of their pain. We can then help empower those with seemingly little

---

[5] The 18th century British statesman, Edmund Burke is often credited with this quote, yet the actual source is unknown.
[6] Proverbs 31:8-9.

power to advocate for their own cause. We can assure them of their God given right to do so, and go before them to prepare the hearts and minds of Spirit-awakened people to hear.

The adage, "when you see something, say something," may be cliché, yet it admonishes us to address situations where we come face to face with injustice, articulating what those who cannot speak out for themselves would say to those who will not hear them. Those in positions where their voices can heard, must speak truth to power authentically, consistently, and with conviction on behalf of those whose voices have been silenced.

Influence

Our example of justice-seeking goes a long way in encouraging people in our lives who intentionally or unintentionally see and hear us to do the same. In wielding influence, what we don't do is as important as what we do. Our role in such efforts can be as broad as helping strategically positioned people make ethical choices, encouraging them to avoid denigrating gestures or language even in jest and creating safe places for others to be heard and empowering them to want to speak.

Inviting those targets of bias into your circle, signals to them and others the importance of such inclusion. Showing specific ways justice-seeking has benefitted communities allows others to imagine how it can benefit them. Developing and demonstrating courageous consistency, even in the face of rejection and ridicule, exemplifies the role of conviction.

Social change agents are effective because they don't give up. Passionate, determined devotion to a just cause can be contagious and move others to speak or act.

Action

Just as Paul admonishes that loveless faith is in authentic, James is adamant that "faith without works"—action—"is dead"[7] and "useless."[8] What matters is what we, as Spirit-renewed Christians, are willing to do about seeking justice? Do we continue dismissing the project as a fad or leave it to the pursuit of those we consider radical fanatics while we complain about tactics we consider unscriptural? Or do we embrace the mandate to all God's people to seek justice? Naming justice as social doesn't remove that mandate for we were created as social beings to be in God-ordained relationship with each other. So, finally, we must admit that we are speaking of biblical—rather than social—justice.

Claude Alexander, calls Christian leaders to be critical reconcilers, noting that we must continuously critique what is wrong or unjust at the same time we work to show a different way to be in relationship with the other.[9] As Spirit-empowered Christians, we have identified that we are fully equipped to do just that if we avail ourselves of the tools at our disposal. The mantle of pneumatological unction, our sense of pneumatological urgency, and our claim to prophetic audacity equip us for that. Yet, we must choose whether to employ them on behalf of God's project or allow them to lie dormant as we critique and complain about the rhetoric and actions of others.

---

[7] James 2:26.
[8] James 2:20.
[9] See, for example, Claude R. Alexander Jr., *Necessary Christianity: What Jesus Shows We Must Be and Do*. Downers Grove, IL: InterVarsity Press, 2022 and Claude Alexander and Mac Pier, *Required: God's Call to Justice, Mercy, and Humility to Overcome Racial Division*. New York: Movement Day Publishing, 2021.

Using Robert Clarence Lawson's "Prayer for Freedom from Race Prejudice" as a model, let us intreat God for the gift of courage to stand against all injustice!

> O God, who has made man in thine own likeness, and who doth love all whom Thou has made, suffer us not because of difference of race, color, or condition to separate ourselves from others and thereby from Thee; but teach us the unity of Thy family and universality of Thy Love. As Thou Savior, as a Son, was born of an Hebrew mother, who had the blood of many nations in her veins; and ministered first to Thy brethren of the Israelites, but rejoiced in the faith of a Syro-Phoenician woman and of a Roman soldier, and suffered your cross to be carried by an Ethiopian; teach us, also, while loving and serving our own, to enter into the communion of the whole family; and forbid that from pride of birth, color, achievement and hardness of heart, we should despise any for whom Christ died, or injure or grieve any in whom He lives. We pray in Jesus' precious name. AMEN[10]

---

[10] Robert Clarence Lawson, "Prayer for Freedom from Race Prejudice" in James Melvin Washington, ed., *Conversations with God: Two Centuries of Prayers by African Americans.* New York: HarperPerennial, 1995, 143.

Bibliography

"Catechism: The Church of the Living God," <www.mc.maricopa.edu/~kefir/club/african_ american/index.html>.

Aldred, Joe D. *Respect: Understanding Caribbean British Christianity.* Epworth, UK: Peterborough, Press, 2005.

Alexander, Estrelda. *The Will to Power: Confronting the Ideologies that Dismantle Christian Community.* Capitol Heights, MD: Seymour Press, 2020.

_____."When Liberation Becomes Survival" *Pnuema,* (Fall 2012), 337-353.

Agosto, Efraín. "Scripture and Liberating Ethics: Honoring Eldin Villafañe" Lexington Theological Quarterly, (2018), 59-67.//.

Anderson, Arthur M, ed. *For The Defense of The Gospel: Writings of Bishop R.C. Lawson.* New York, NY: Church of Our Lord Jesus Christ, 1972.

Baer; Hans A and Merrill Singer. *African-American Religion in the Twentieth Century: Varieties of Protest And Accommodation.* Knoxville, TN: University of Tennessee Press, 1997.

Bridges-Johns, Cheryl. *Finding Eternal Treasures.* Cleveland, TN: Pathway Press, 1986.

_____. Pentecostal Formation: A Pedagogy Among the Oppressed. Eugene, OR: Wipf and Stock, 2010.

Brueggemann, Walter. *The Prophetic Imagination.* Minneapolis: Fortress Press, 1978.

Daughtry, Herbert. No Monopoly on Suffering: Blacks and Jews in Crown Heights and Elsewhere. Trenton, NJ: Africa World Press, 1997.

Davies, Andrew. The spirit of freedom: Pentecostals, the Bible and Social Justice" *Journal of the European Pentecostal Theological Association*, 31 no 1 (2011), 53-64.

Dayton, Donald W. "Pentecostal/Charismatic Renewal And Social Change: A Western Perspective" *Transformation* 5:4 (1988), 7-13.

Dempster, Murray W. "The Church's Moral Witness: A Study of Glossolalia in Luke's Theology of Acts" *Paraclete* 23 (1989), 1-7.

_____. "Eschatology, Spirit baptism, and inclusiveness: an exploration into the hallmarks of a Pentecostal social ethic" in Peter Althouse and Robby Waddell eds., *Perspectives in Pentecostal Eschatologies: World without End,* Eugene, OR: Pickwick Publications, 2010, 155-188.

Forbes, Jr., James A. "Shall We Call This Dream Progressive Pentecostalism" *Spirit* 1:1 (1977), 12-17.

_____. *The Holy Spirit and Preaching*. Nashville, TN: Abingdon Press, 1989.

Franklin, Robert. *Liberating Visions: Human Fulfillment and Social Justice in African American Thought*. Minneapolis: Fortress Press, 1989.

_____. *Another Day's Journey: Black Churches Confronting the American Crisis*. Minneapolis: Fortress Press, 1997.

Goodwin, Bennie, "Social Implications of Pentecostal Power" *Spirit* 1:1, (1977), 31-35.

Grenz, Stanley J. *Welcoming but Not Affirming: An Evangelical Response to Homosexuality*. Philadelphia: Westminster John Knox Press, 1998.

Hill, Elijah L. *The Missing Link of the American Civil Rights Movement: The Pre-Civil Rights Contribution of Bishop C.H. Mason*. S.l.: Createspace, 2016.

Hollenweger, Walter. "Black Pentecostal Concept," *Concept 30*. Geneva, Switzerland: World Council of Churches, 1970, 16-19.

Hundley, Raymond. *Radical Liberation Theology: An Evangelical Response*. Wilmore, KY: Bristol Books, 1987.

Irvin, Dale T. "Drawing all Together in One Bond of Love: The Ecumenical Vision of William J. Seymour and the Azusa Street Revival," *Journal of Pentecostal Theology*, 6 (1995), 25-53.

Israel, Adrienne. *Amanda Berry Smith: From Washerwoman to Evangelist.*, Lanham, MD: Scarecrow Press, 1998.

Jefferson, Anita Bingham. (Charles Price Jones First Black Holiness Reformer with a One Hundred Year Chronology of His Life, Florence, MS: Stephens Printing, 2011.

Jones, Charles Price. *An Appeal to the Sons of Africa: A Number of Poems, Readings, Orations and Lectures, Designed Especially to Inspire Youth of African Blood with Sentiments of Hope and Nobility as well as to Entertain and Instruct all Classes of Readers and Lovers of Humanity*. Jackson, MS. Truth Publishing Company, 1902.

Keener, Craig S. "Some New Testament Invitations to Ethnic Reconciliation" *Evangelical Quarterly*. 75:3, (2003), 195–213.

_____. "Women in Ministry: Another Egalitarian Perspective" in James R. Beck, ed., *Two Views on Women in Ministry*, Grand Rapids, MI: Zondervan Academic, 2005.

_____. and Médine Moussounga Keener. *Impossible Love: The True Story of an African Civil War, Miracles and Hope Against All Odd.*, Ada, MI: Chosen Books, 2016.

Kärkkäinen, Veli-Matti. Are Pentecostals oblivious to social justice?: theological and ecumenical perspectives" *Missiology* 29:4 (2001), 417-431.

Mamiya, Lawrence H. A Social History of Bethel African Methodist Episcopal Church in Baltimore: The House of God and the Struggle for Freedom" in James P. Wind and James Welborn Lewis, eds. *American Congregations: Portraits of Twelve Religious Communities*, Chicago: The University of Chicago Press, 1994, 266.

Miller, Donald and Tetsunao Yamamori. *Global Pentecostalism: The New Face of Christian Social Engagement*, Oakland, CA: University of California Press; 2007.

Roberts, J. Deotis. *Black Theology in Dialog*, Philadelphia: Westminster Press, 1987.

Robinson, Ida. The Economic Persecution. *Latter Day Messenger.* (May 3, 1935), 2.

Rohane, Kyle. "Ministry after a Fatal Police Shooting" *Christianity Today* October 3, 2016.

Samuel Solivan. *Spirit, Pathos and Liberation: Toward an Hispanic Pentecostal Theology* (Journal of Pentecostal Theology Supplement) New York: Bloomsbury T&T Clark, 1998.

Schussler Fiorenza, Elisabeth. *The Book of Revelation: Justice and Judgment.* Minneapolis: Fortress Press, 1998.

Smith, Amanda Berry. *An Autobiography: The Story of the Lord's Dealings with Mrs. Amanda Smith, the Colored Evangelist: Containing an Account of Her Life Work of Faith, and Her Travels in America, England, Ireland, Scotland, India, and Africa as an Independent Missionary.* Chicago: Meyer & Brother Publishers, 1893..

Spellman, Robert C. *Facts and Photos About Our Founders: Bishop R.C. Lawson and Mother Carrie F. Lawson. Gainesville*, FL: Displays For Schools, Inc., 1998.

Spellman, Robert C, and Mabel L. Thomas. *The Life, Legend And Legacy of Bishop R. C. Lawson.* Scotch Plains, NJ: Privately Printed, 1983.

Stewart, Alexander C. *Add Thou to It: The Selected Works of Robert Clarence Lawson*, Capitol Heights, MD: Seymour Press, 2020.

Stewart, Alexander C and Sherry Sherrod DuPree. *The Silent Spokesman: Bishop Robert Clarence Lawson.* Gainesville, FL: Displays For Schools, Inc., 1994.

Stone, Howard K. and James O. Duke. *How to Think Theologically,* 2nd Edition. Minneapolis: Fortress Press, 2006.

Villafañe, Eldin. Seek the Peace of the City: Reflections on Urban Ministry (Grand Rapids, MI: William B. Eerdmans, 1995.

_____. *The Liberating Spirit: Toward an Hispanic American Pentecostal Social Ethic.* Rapids, MI: Wm. B. Eerdmans, 1993.

Warrington, Keith. "Social Transformation in the Missions of Pentecostals: A Priority or a Bonus?" *European Pentecostal Theological Association.* 31:1 (2011), 17-35.

Williams, Smallwood E. *Significant Sermons.* Washington, DC, Bible Way Church, 1971.

_____ *This is my Story: A Significant Life Struggle.* Washington, DC: William Willoughby Publishers, 1981.

Yong, Amos. *In the Days of Caesar: Pentecostalism & Political Theology.* Grand Rapids, MI: Wm B. Eerdmans, 2010.

_____. "Justice Deprived, Justice Demanded: Afropentecostalisms and the Task of World Pentecostal Theology Today," *Journal of Pentecostal Theology* 15:1 [2006], 130.

Zehr, Howard. *The Little Book of Restorative Justice,* Intercourse, PA: Good Books 2005.

Zerbe, Gordon. "Revelation's Exposé of Two Cities: Babylon and New Jerusalem" *Direction* 32:1 (Spring 2003), 47–60.

Index

Abolition, 103-104, 147, 161
Abortion, 186-187
Abraham, ii, 105
Accommodationist strategies, 9, 154-158
Activism, 9, 110, 124, 125, 134, 160-166, 193-194, 197
    Radical, 161-164
    Strategic, 160-161
African People's Christian Organization, 124
Ahab, 35
AIDS, 96, 124
Aldred, Joe, 127
Alexander, Claude, 183, 201
Ali, Abiy, 127
Alinsky, Sol, 117
Amanda Smith Orphanage and Industrial Home for Abandoned and Destitute Colored Children, 107
American Anti-slavery Society, 103
Amnon, 35
Amos, 51-53, 179
Angelus Temple, 121
Apartheid, 125, 162
Apostolic Overcoming Holy Church of God, 112-113

Azusa Street Revival, iv, 8, 83-86, 89, 105, 107-108, 119, 122, 149, 153, 162, 184, 190, 191

Bartleman, Frank, 88, 108
Beckford, Robert, 9, 137
Berry, Bill, 117
Bewley, Anthony, 104
Bible Way Church of Our Lord Jesus Christ World Wide, 116
Bonhoeffer, Dietrich, 190
Brazier, Arthur, 9, 95, 116-117, 162
Bridges Johns, Cheryl, 134-135
Bryant, John Richard, 150-151

Catholic social teaching, 148-149
Center for Urban Ministerial Education, 134
Centre for Black and White Christian Partnership, 127
Charismatic movement, 94
Charles H. Mason Theological Seminary, 133
Chicago Urban League, 117
Chikane, Frank, 125-126, 162
Christian, William, 105-106
Church of Christ Bible Institute, 115

Church of God (Anderson, IN), 104, *see also* Evening Light Saints
Church of God (Cleveland, TN), 117
Church of God in Christ (COGIC), 89, 106, 109-112, 120, 132
Church of Christ (Holiness) USA, 106
Church of God of Prophecy, 117, 127
Church of Our Lord Jesus Christ of the Apostolic Faith, 115
Church of the Living God (Christian Workers for Fellowship), 105
Civil Rights Movement, 102-113, 115, 124-125. 162, 191
classical Pentecostals, iii, v, 21, 92, 94, 100, 101, 102, 124,
Clemmons, Ithiel, 110, 111, 190
Clemmons, Joseph, 111
Commission on Faith and Order for the National Council of Churches, 135
Community Justice Reform Coalition, 125
Conservative Christians, 6, 19, 76, 80 *see also,* Evangelicalism
Cook, Mozella, 120
Coordinating Council of Community Organizations, 117

Daniel, 50
Darius, 50
Daughters of Zelophehad, 29-30
Daughtry, Herbert, 9, 124, 162
David, 32, 35
Dempster, Murray, 135
Duke, James O., 100
Dinkins, David N., 125

Ecclesiastes, 41- 42, 199
Edwards, Joel, 127
Esther, 32, 36-37, 165
Ethiopian Eunuch, 78
Ethiopian Orthodox Church, 126
Ethiopian Overcoming Holy Church of God, *see* Apostolic Overcoming Holy Church of God
Ethiopian World Federation, 115
Ethiopianism, 113
Evangelicals and Catholics Together (ECT), 135
Evangelicalism, 141-144
and justice, 122, 128, 136, 172, 195
Evening Light Saints, 104-105
Ezekiel, 49-50
Ezra, 32, 36

Farrow, Lucy, 84, 118
First March on Washington, 115
Forbes, James A Jr., 4-5, 123-124
Ford, Louis, 110, 111-112
Floyd, George, iv
Franklin, Robert, 9, 133-134
Free Methodist Church, 134
Fund for Community Redevelopment and Revitalization, 117

Garr, Alfred and Lillian, 84
Garrison, William Lloyd, 103
Good Samaritan, 2, 69
Goodwin, Bennie, 9, 132
Gospels 61-74

Habakkuk, 56-57
Haggai, 50
Haman, 35-36
Haven, Gilbert, 103
Haywood, Garfield T., 114-115
Heschel, Abraham Joshua, i
Hoffman, Nicholas Von, 117
Holiness Movement, iii. 1, 6, 83, 88, 92, 102-107, 119, 128, 130, 147, 164
Homosexuality, 96,132, 184-186
Horn, Rosa Artemis, 87, 120, 122
Houghton College, 103
House of the Lord Churches, 124

Human Rights and Social Justice Program at the Ford Foundation, 133-134

Image of Christ, 11
image of God, ii, iii, 8, 15, 74, 148, 157-158, 173-174, 175, 184,186, 189, 190, 194, 195
Industrial Areas Foundation, 116
International Roman Catholic-Pentecostal Dialogue, 132
Isaiah, 44-47
Israel, 2, 7, 27-59, 69, 72, 73, 174, see also Northern Kingdom or Southern Kingdom

Jackson, Jesse, 124
James, 78-79
Jeremiah, 47-49, 179
Jesus, iii, 5, 6, 7,13, 22, 60, 61-69, 72-73, 74, 77, 78, 83, 84,86-87, 94, 105, 113, 118-119, 141, 142, 151, 156, 163, 164, 165, 172, 173, 181, 187, 189-190, 194,
Jezebel, 35
Jim Crow Era, 161-162
Job, 42-44
Joel, 50, 51, 75, 83, 182
John, 74, 80, 142
Jonah, 50, 54-57
Jones, Charles Price, 106
Joseph, 28

Judah, 28

Keener, Craig, 134
King, Jr., Martin Luther, 117, 190
Kingdom of God, iii, 3, 4-5, 11, 61, 63-66, 72, 73, 76, 82, 83, 100-101, 113-114, 127, 128-129, 142, 149-150, 151, 152, 156, 168, 169, 170, 171, 172-, 178, 184, 188-189, 194, 195, 198
Ku Klux Klan, 114-115

Lamentations, 41
Lambert, Eva, 120
Lawson, Robert Clarence, 114-115-116, 202
Lawsonville, 115
LGBQT community, 75, 125, 175, 183,185,187
Liberal theology, 149-150
Lighthouse Institute for Foursquare Evangelism (L.I.F.E.) Bible College. 121
LIVE FREE Campaign. 125
Lovett, Leonard, 9, 133
Luke, 65, 68-69, 72
Luther, Martin, 190

MacRobert, Iain, 101-102
Malachi, 51, 58-60
Malcolm X, 115

Mandella, Nelson and Winnie, 125
Mark, 142
Mason, Charles Harrison (C.H.), 9, 109-110
Matthew, 64, 142
McBride, Michael, 125
McKinney, George, 153, 190-191
McPherson, Aimee Semple, 87, 120-121
Methodist Episcopal Church, 103
Methodist Episcopal Church South, 104

Micah, 55-56
Miller, Donald,4-5, 124
Miriam, 29
Misogyny, 58, 70, 183, 185, 188, 195
mishpat, i-iv, 26, 27
Mordechai, 37
Morehouse College, 133
Moses, 29-31, 60, 68, 81, 164
Mount Sinai Holy Church, 120
Mukwege, Denis, 126

Nahum, 50, 55
Naomi, 37
Nation of Islam, 115
National Association of Black Evangelicals, 132

National Black Brown Gun Violence Prevention Consortium, 125
Nehemiah, 35-36
Niemuller, Martin, 190
Neo-Pentecostalism, 1, 6, 89, 94, 129, 130, 135
New Testament Church of God, 137
Nobel Peace Prize, 126-127
Northern Kingdom, 44, 52

Obadiah, 53-54, 169
Oberlin College, 103
Operation Breadbasket, 124

Pacifism, 109
Panzi Hospital, 126
Parham, Charles, 108
Patterson, James O., 110, 112
Paul, 60, 62, 75-78, 151-152, 163, 164, 166-167, 173, 197, 180, 201
Pentecostal Assemblies of the World, 89, 114
Peter, 78
Pharisees, 64, 68, 72
Phillips, William T., 112-113
Pillar of Fire, 108
Pneumatological unction, 10, 1661-166, 177, 182, 189, 191, 194, 201,

Pneumatological urgency, 10, 166, 171--177, 178, 182, 184, 185, 189, 191, 194, 201
Powell, Adam Clayton, Jr., 115
Prophetic audacity, 11, 166, 178-184, 185, 188, 188, 191,194, 198, 201
Prophets, the, ii, iii, 7, 25, 26, 35, 43-60, 64, 68, 78-80, 179-180
    Major, 44-50
    Minor, 50-60
Proverbs, 40
Psalms, i, 20, 37-40

R.C. Lawson Institute, 115
Raby, Al, 117
reconciliation, 74, 191
    humanity, 78,
    racial, 109, 111, 134
    with God, 1, 41
Reems, Ernestine Cleveland, 120-121
Reform strategies, 9, 158-160
Riverside Church, 123-124
Roberts, J. Deotis, 94-95, 101-102
Robinson, Ida Bell, 9, 87, 120
Rousseau, Leoncia Rosado, 121-122
Ruth, 37

Salvation Army, 108
Samaritan Women, 68, 74., 94

Scandrett-Leatherman, Craig, 134
Scribes, 64
Secretary for Minority Ethnic Christian Affairs (MECA) at Churches Together in England, 127
Selassie, Haile, 115-116
Seymour, William Joseph, iv, 9, 84-86, 105, 107-108, 118-119, 133, 152
Sharpton Jr., Alfred Charles (Al), 111
slavery
    global, 174-175, 176
    in America, 17, 75, 103-104, 114, 147, 156,161,162, 163
    in the Bible, 28, 52, 164-165

Smith, Amanda Berry. 106-107, 119
Smith, Elias Dempsey, 113-114
Smith, Lucy Madden, 122
Solivan, Samuel, 135-136
Sought Out Church of God in Christ, 120
South Africa, 125, 126,
South African Council of Churches (SACC), 126
Southern Christian Leadership Conference, 116, 132
Southern Kingdom, 44, 52

speaking in tongues, 83-84, 87, 92-93, 99, 135, 151, 152
Spirit-empowerment, 5, 8, 10, 25, 66, 74, 82-83, 91, 94, 95-96, 112, 117, 119, 122, 138,146-148, 150-152, 155, 165, 167, 168, 171, 178, 182, 183, 189, 190-191, 193, 195, 198-199, 201
spiritual gifts, 93-94
Stone, Howard W., 100
Sunderland, Leroy, 103

Tamar
    Judah's daughter-in-law, 28
    David's daughter, 35
Tate, Mary Magdalena, 87, 120
Temporary Woodlawn Organization (TWO), 117
Thornton, Mattie, 87
Tinney, James S. 132-133
Tomlinson, Ambrose Jessup (A.J.), 117-118
Triumph the Church and Kingdom of God, 113-114
tzedakah, i-iv, 26-27, 62

Underground Railroad. 162, 163
United Holy Church of America, 118, 122
University of Chicago, 117
Urban EcoBlock The, 134

Valdez, Susie, 122
Vatican, 70, 124-125
Villafañe, Eldin, 136

Waddles, Charleszetta, 123
Warner, Daniel S., 104-105
Washington, Frederick, 110-111
Wesleyan Methodist Church, 103
White, Alma, 108, 120
Williams, Smallwood, 116
Wisdom Literature, 40-43
Women, 85-87, 118-122, 134, 136,
  174-175, 187
  and Jesus, 68, 74, 86,
  in scripture, 30, 77
  ministers, 8, 9, 87, 118-122
Woodlawn Preservation and
  Investment Corporation, 117

xenolalia, 83-84

Yamamori, Tetsunao, 4-5, 124
Yong, Amos, 100

Zechariah, 50, 57-58
Zephaniah 50, 58

www.ingramcontent.com/pod-product-compliance
Lightning Source LLC
Chambersburg PA
CBHW050315120526
44592CB00014B/1919